NAMIBIA
THE RAVAGES OF WAR

South Africa's onslaught on the Namibian People

by

Barbara König

INTERNATIONAL DEFENSE & AID FUND
for Southern Africa
P. O. BOX 17
CAMBRIDGE, MA. 02138

International Defence and Aid Fund for Southern Africa
104 Newgate Street London EC1
1983

The International Defence and Aid Fund for South Africa is a humanitarian organisation which has worked consistently for peaceful and constructive solutions to the problems created by racial oppression in South Africa.

It sprang from Christian and humanist opposition to the evils and injustices of apartheid in South Africa. It is dedicated to the achievement of free, democratic, non-racial societies throughout Southern Africa.

The objects of the Fund are:—

(i) to aid, defend and rehabilitate the victims of unjust legislation and oppressive and arbitrary procedures,

(ii) to support their families and dependents,

(iii) to keep the conscience of the world alive to the issues at stake.

In accordance with these three objects, the Fund distributes its humanitarian aid to the victims of racial injustice without any discrimination on the grounds of race, colour, religious or political affiliation. The only criterion is that of genuine need.

For many years, under clause (iii) of its objects, The Fund has run a comprehensive information service on affairs in Southern Africa. This includes visual documentation. It produces a regular news bulletin 'FOCUS' on Political Repression in Southern Africa, and publishes pamphlets and books on all aspects of life in Southern Africa.

The fund prides itself on the strict accuracy of all its information.

ISBN No. 0 904759 51 2

Printed in England by Shadowdean Ltd. London

Contents

INTRODUCTION

The Namibian people are living under the occupation of a foreign army. An estimated 100,000 troops controlled by the South African Defence Force, supported by approximately 10,000 police, are illegally stationed in a country whose population is officially given as 1,009,000.[1] They remain there in defiance of the United Nation's (UN) termination of South Africa's Mandate over Namibia in 1966, of the UN Security Council's resolution in 1969 declaring South Africa's continued presence in Namibia illegal, and of the International Court of Justice ruling to the same effect in 1971. This massive military presence is the main instrument in South Africa's efforts to preserve the power of the white minority in the territory, and thus retain the last white-dominated buffer between the apartheid Republic and the black independent states to the north, notably Angola. It backs up a South African-controlled administration in Namibia whose policies reflect those of South Africa itself, denying the black majority the right to self-determination and independence. How does this military occupation affect the lives of the black civilian population of Namibia?

In a letter to a Namibian newspaper in early 1981, one reader described the situation prevailing in the north of the country:

> 'Today's stories from the north are incredible . . . They tell of villages *(sic)* being rounded up and men and women of all ages being made to lie on their stomachs in long queues for hours on end; innocent people beaten up mercilessly, even after having produced the required documents; houses burnt down to ashes, people asked to surrender their bicycles, radios, cassette players or watches never to get them back. People from the north also tell of starvation of detainees, particularly at a transit camp at Outapi in Ombalantu.
>
> Today many Namibian men and women spend sleepless nights because of the plight of our country and our people.[2]

Accounts such as this one have been supported by numerous other reports of the devastating effect of South Africa's war on the civilian population in Namibia. One prominent church leader, Dr. Paul Wee, wrote in 1979, after a brief visit to Namibia:

> 'The evidence of suffering is everywhere—the shattered wrecks of cars, the graves of many victims, usually innocent farmers and children. Hundreds of stories one hears these days of intimidation, torture, detention and death, primarily at the hands of South African army units . . .
>
> The constant element in the present situation is fear. This is not only in evidence in the villages and kraals of the northern areas or

the Tsumeb countryside where the heaviest fighting takes place, but among the common people, the church leaders, school teachers and hospital personnel, especially in Ovamboland.[3]

It is clear from all available evidence that South Africa's military onslaught has inflicted profound damage on the socio-ecomomic structures of Namibian society. The black majority, exploited as cheap labour by the white minority, and deprived of political and economic power by apartheid rule, have experienced the virtual destruction of their way of life. The cost of the damage inflicted by this armed occupation, while at present unquantifiable, appears to be enormous in both human and material terms.

Military censorship of the press makes it difficult to obtain information, thus creating problems in building up an overall picture of the scale of the damage. Black Namibians have few means to convey their plight to the outside world, and risk retribution if they expose South African repression. Consequently, many reports in recent years have come from foreign visitors to the country, notably from church delegations, who have interviewed numerous black civilians and described the climate of terror among the population. Evidence has been accumulated of the destruction of crops and fences by the army, of forcible population removals to prevent civilian support for the liberation movement, the South West Africa People's Organisation (SWAPO), and of the destruction of the supply networks for goods and food due to curfews and mined roads. They give an indication of the widespread breakdown of essential services. Hospitals, schools and other social services are also affected, with shortage of personnel and difficulty of access due to the war reducing their already rudimentary facilities still further.

The pervasive military presence, the brutal behaviour of the security forces and their deliberate assault on the deeply held beliefs and conventions of the local population, penetrate deeply into the fabric of Namibian society. Families are broken up as a result of military operations, children and elderly people may be left completely alone after their relatives have been killed. Many arrive in the refugee settlements in Angola in a state of profound psychological shock and trauma.[4] People see their dead desecrated by soldiers who drive around with the bodies of suspected SWAPO guerillas dangling from army trucks.[5] According to a report by a visiting church delegation in 1982, it is 'commonly accepted that in searching out SWAPO guerillas the security forces stop at nothing to force information out of people'.[6]

The destructive role of the South African security forces and their local recruits stands in contrast to the efforts being made, under the auspices of the liberation movement, SWAPO, towards building a new society for an independent Namiba. Under South African occupation, black Namibians have been deprived of adequate education, health care, access to skilled jobs and other basic rights. In the refugee settlements and elsewhere, SWAPO has created new structures to enable Namibians to control their own lives, to work co-operatively, and to learn skills needed for the future. For an

6

estimated 73,000 Namibians[7] forced into exile by South Africa's repressive policies, this is their first experience of freedom from persecution and racial discrimination.

For those living in the territory the experience of repression by the South African security forces has resulted in the hardening of their resolve to resist South African occupation. This is shown in the persistent courage and defiance which the population displays in the face of repression, and in the overwhelming commitment, documented by Namibian and foreign observers alike, to the liberation of Namibia from South African rule, through support for SWAPO.[8] Numerous acts of resistance to and non-cooperation with the security forces, and an underground network of information and help for the guerillas, show clearly where the sympathies of the majority of the people lie.

South Africa's Mandate over Namibia, conferred in 1919 by the League of Nations, was terminated in 1966 by the United Nations. South Africa nevertheless remains in Namibia, in defiance of the UN and the International Court of Justice. It has installed a white-controlled administration, headed by a 'government' loyal to Pretoria, and controlled by a South African-appointed Administrator General. It has enlarged its military presence by establishing new military bases and rapidly increasing the number of troops in the territory. These are used to control the Namibian civilian population, to counter the growing effectiveness of SWAPO's armed struggle, and to mount virtually daily attacks and reconnaissance missions into Angola across the Namibian border. Fear of and hostility towards the independent state of Angola, which repelled a large-scale South African invasion of its territory in 1975/76, plays a major part in the massive concentration of South African troops in the north of Namibia. Angolan independence in 1975 enabled SWAPO to intensify its armed struggle, launched in 1966, and thus threaten South Africa's hold on the territory more effectively.

This Fact Paper deals with the military aspect of South Africa's illegal presence in Namibia. While the civilian administration has implemented the racial policies which institutionalise the exploitation of the black majority, the pervasive military presence has underpinned these structures and has increasingly become the dominant force.[9] The Fact Paper presents factual evidence, collected from numerous accounts of victims of violence, from churches, visiting journalists, the local press, and court cases, of the consequences of South Africa's military occupation on the lives of black Namibians. Specific incidents of brutality by the security forces, mass shootings of civilians, arbitrary searches and destruction of villages, detention and torture of individuals, are too numerous to be comprehensively listed. Examples of such incidents are used to illustrate the general state of repression that exists throughout Namibia, and to give an idea of how people live under such conditions.

The evidence presented in this Fact Paper leads to the conclusion that South Africa's rule has not achieved its aim of subduing the population into accepting South African rule. On the contrary, support for SWAPO has grown as South African soldiers and police have clearly shown their indifference to the suffering they inflict on all segments of the Namibian population. Until Namibia achieves genuine independence, this situation is likely to intensify.

I LIVING UNDER MILITARY OCCUPATION

'Every few miles along the side of the road there is an army camp . . . The heavily tarred road was absolutely full of South African military vehicles and personnel . . . There are prisons in every town as well . . . The Namibian people are being *protected to death* by the South Africans'.[1]

The Process of Militarisation

South Africa's military strategy in Namibia has been conditioned by the guerilla struggle waged by the People's Liberation Army of Namibia (PLAN), the military wing of SWAPO. This intensified dramatically following Angolan independence in 1975. PLAN combatants were able to extend their activities by crossing the Angolan-Namibian border and to operate along a front almost 1,000 miles long across northern Namibia. They were able to establish guerilla training bases and SWAPO refugee settlements in Angola.[2]

South Africa's aim has been to separate SWAPO from the local population in Namibia and thus prevent any civilian assistance to the liberation movement. This has involved the creation of a *cordon sanitaire* along the border between Angola and Namibia. During 1981, this buffer zone was extended through the occupation by South African troops of substantial parts of southern Angola, following a large-scale invasion of the country in August of that year.[3] In addition, the Namibian black population in the north has been forced into 'protected villages' guarded by South African military personnel, and subjected to numerous restrictions and repressive measures.

The presence of South African military and para-military forces has, as a consequence of these measures, fundamentally transformed the way of life of black Namibians. Their existence has been ruled by the 'security needs' as defined by the South African authorities, and their daily survival has scarcely figured in the military strategies of the apartheid regime. Whole villages have been removed from areas designated as free-fire zones and relocated close to, but fenced off from, 'white' bases, while the civilian population has been subjected to systematic police and army violence. The civilian response has, in many reported cases, been one of quiet resistance and continued support for SWAPO, and growing hostility to the army's presence. South Africa's military blanket over the north of Namibia has failed to crush PLAN activities, which have in fact penetrated further south into the 'white' farming region of central Namibia.

South Africa's military presence in Namibia expanded rapidly in the 1970s following the arrival of South African Defence Force (SADF) personnel in the territory in 1972 to help the South African Police (SAP) suppress a general strike by Namibian workers. By 1974, troop strength had grown to approximately 15,000 while by 1976, following the South African invasion of Angola in 1975, an estimated 45,000 troops were stationed in Namibia. By September 1980, this had almost doubled to between 70 and 80,000 and reached 100,000 in April 1981.[4]

The Namibian population found that during this period, an increasing number of military bases were being built, transforming their villages into armed garrisons and destroying their livelihood which had depended on the land now gradually being taken over by the army. From three bases in the early 1960s in Windhoek, Walvis Bay and the Eastern Caprivi, South African installations multiplied to an estimated 40 bases along the northern border with Angola and another 35 in the rest of the country in 1980.[5] The South African army took over office blocks in Windhoek in March 1979, and bought land covering 60,000 hectares in the area around Okahandja in central Namibia to expand an existing base and erect a training college.[6] A military base south of Windhoek was enlarged in 1980,[7] and another base covering 860 hectares was established in the same area in June 1981.[8]

As a result, Namibians were increasingly forced to live under the constant surveillance of the South African military forces, close to but outside the fortified towns. A group of journalists visiting the north of Namibia in August 1980 conveyed their impression of the fortress-like appearance of these bases. At Katima Mulilo, in Eastern Caprivi, they noted 'bombshelters in every backyard and a security fence under construction around the settlement'.[10] Towns on or near the border with Angola, such as Rundu, Oshakati and Katima Mulilo had 'miniscule white populations who virtually all worked for the South African government'.[11]

Reporting on a visit to the north in 1981, a British journalist found the military camps 'bigger, better fortified and better equipped' than on a previous visit and noted that the number of military vehicles had substantially increased. He described the bases as 'heavily defended, with an air of permanency about them'.[12]

According to another report, the South African army occupied nearly every village and controlled nearly every town in the Ovambo region.

> 'All towns like Ondangwa and Oshakati, but also small communities like Ongwediva, Oshigambo, Oniipa and Otjimbingwe, where church institutions are located, are surrounded by barbed wire fences with sentries of the Home Guard (tribal police) and the South African army standing at the single entrance. In addition, armoured personnel carriers and army troops are everywhere, and in great numbers',

the visitor reported. He described Ondangwa, once a quiet palmtree-laced village in Ovambo, as 'a military fortress occupied by tanks, armoured personnel carriers, underground bunkers and perhaps ten thousand South African soldiers'. Inside the town 'the feeling was one of imprisonment with heavy military equipment and high barricades of concrete, sand and barbed wire all round'.[13]

What happened to the communities who had been invaded by this foreign military might, ostensibly for their own protection? According to a church delegation visiting Namibia in late 1981, the visitors were told again and again by Namibians: 'These people (the army) are supposed to be protecting us. Against whom do we need to be protected? Would to God someone would protect us against these so-called protectors!'[14]

Forced Removals

In the mid-1970s, a systematic programme of forced removals was carried out by South African forces in the north of Namibia. A one kilometre wide strip was due to be cleared of all human presence to create a free-fire zone along the entire border between Angola and Namibia. The purpose of the operation was to separate SWAPO forces in Angola from the local population in Namibia, and allow for more effective patrolling of the border. As a result, thousands of people lost their homes and livelihood. When preparations for the establishment of this buffer zone began in Ocober 1975, it was claimed that less than 100 civilians in the Kwanyama Tribal Authority would be affected.[15] The evacuation was described by the authorities as a tactical move to safeguard the lives and property of local residents.[16]

As the removals got under way, it became evident that entire villages, kraals, shops, cafes and other businesses were affected. An Anglican vicar who had previously been stationed at Odibo on the northern Namibian border warned that the removals would cause mass dislocation and splitting of families, particularly for the very large number of Ovambos with relatives in Angola. He told a United Nations committee that five church centres, two hospitals and several schools would have to be abandoned and that the Ovambo people would forfeit the use of the best watered farmland in the region.[17]

As the clearance operation for the one kilometre strip continued, reports spoke of the wholesale destruction of villages and crops. In 1976, the UN Commissioner for Namibia estimated that South African troops had uprooted between 40 and 50 thousand villagers in the previous three months.[18] Namibians who had fled to Angola reported that South African troops were being helped by civilian-driven bulldozers which flattened houses. People who had earlier volunteered for resettlement had been paid some compensation, but this had ceased and eviction was now being conducted by force.[19] In July 1976, the bantustan leader of Ovambo, Pastor Cornelius Ndjoba, issued an order to the security forces to shoot and kill anyone found in the depopulated zone.[20] These measures effectively divided the Ovambo people, who live on both sides of the border, into separate communities, unable to continue the social interaction that had existed for many years.

Once the border clearance was completed, further measures were taken by the South African military to force civilians to move closer to the military bases in an attempt to prevent assistance to SWAPO guerillas. These measures effectively rendered many people, who had previously been farmers or cattlers herders, destitute and dependent on the army. Reports in 1981 spoke of the destruction of pumps and boreholes to cut off water supplies. In a letter to the *Windhoek Observer*, a resident in the north complained that the South African army vehicles were destroying fences and agricultural vegetation.[21] Another report in 1982 confirmed the devastation in northern Namibia.

'Northern Namibia was once a productive, peaceful agricultural area. During rainy seasons patches of growing millet could be seen everywhere, with fences dividing one cultivated area from the other. Presently there is nothing more of this kind. The millet fields, with or without crops, are raised to the ground by racist South Africa's army trucks. Destitution, hunger, and death are hanging like a huge black cloud over the region.[22]

By the early 1980s, there was a growing body of evidence that the security forces were inflicting long-term damage to the economic infrastructure of Namibia.

A German photographer who travelled in the north in 1981, confirmed that

'between the Namib and the Etosha Game Reserve, and of course the Ovambo-speaking region, only a few of the numerous settlements are still occupied. Life is now concentrated on a few larger centres, mostly near military bases and police stations'.

She claimed that this was because people in the area had great confidence in both army and police.[23] In fact, other reports have noted the hostility of the black population towards the South African occupying force. One American journalist was impressed by 'the black population's incredible hostility towards anybody white', and observed that black people were being daily subjected to humiliations by the South Africans.[24]

Fortified Towns

Civilians have little choice about where and how they live under South African military occupation. The establishment of 'protected villages', which were widely used by the Smith regime in Rhodesia during the liberation struggle, has been part of South Africa's policy to isolate the guerilla forces from the local people upon whom they depend, and to exert complete control over civilian movement. The black townships and compounds next to the military bases are fenced in and surrounded by watchtowers. Oshakati black township for instance, which is situated close to the South African command centre for part of the 'operational area', is surrounded by a high wire fence. A general curfew has been imposed by the South Africans, and people risk getting shot if they move around. In one incident reported to a visitor in February 1981, a ten year old boy who was chasing a donkey was shot and killed.[25] The visitor described the tall communication towers and watchtowers with machine guns which dominate the skyline around the town. A reporter, commenting on the strict security measures in force in 1981, wrote:

> 'At dusk, whites have to retreat behind the double security fence which surrounds the settlement of Oshakati. The only entries to Oshakati are guarded by soldiers who can, if necessary, retreat into bomb-proof shelters. Blacks have to leave Oshakati at night and it becomes an all-white settlement'.[26]

All towns and villages in the Ovambo region were reported in 1979 to be surrounded by barbed wire with sentries posted outside the only entrance.[27] At the entrance to the first settlement in Ovambo, Oshivelo, all blacks have their identity documents checked while whites are waved through. One reporter, witnessing procedures at the numerous road-blocks in Ovambo, discovered that there was one queue for whites and one for blacks. Blacks were routinely asked to take their shirts off to show whether they had rifle strap marks on their shoulders. Some building workers who had been carrying heavy metal pipes were arrested as suspected SWAPO guerillas.[28]

Small remote towns and villages such as Opuwo, an administrative centre in the north west of the territory, have been changed completely by the presence of the army. Opuwo, formerly a remote trading station where the Himba, a nomadic cattle trading people, lived, was described by one foreign visitor as having being turned into a besieged garrison town housing 30 white civilian families.[29] A journalist visiting the town in late 1981 described it as an armed camp characterised by the large presence of Panzer vehicles, and of police and army task forces with sub-machine guns. Eight kilometers to the north west is a huge military base, and at the same distance to the south east is another one.[30]

In the town itself the whites live completely apart from the shanty towns of the black people. As a result of the war, Opuwo's population increased from about 500 in 1979 to around 4,000 in 1981, with many black people living in squatter camps. Having been forced to abandon their villages and possessions, many of the newly arrived families are reported to become dependent on the earnings of sons who have joined the South African army for a steady job.[31]

Local Recruits

Black Namibian civilians find themselves surrounded not only by South African security forces, but by a variety of local forces recruited by South

Africa to give the war a 'local' image. These include black Namibians who have voluntarily, or through economic necessity, joined one of the number of tribally based police and paramilitary units created by South Africa, and those who have been conscripted into the army following the extension of compulsory military service to black Namibians in January 1981. Conscription has affected various sections of the population, including migrant workers and students.

The Home Guards are among the most notorious of the paramilitary forces. They were initially created to protect bantustan leaders and tribal chiefs who co-operated with South Africa. The Home Guards have increasingly used their position to terrorise the local population. One foreign observer described them as 'young black dropouts from Ovambo society... armed bands, often undisciplined, who are known for committing atrocities against their own people'.[32] A report in a Namibian newspaper noted in 1980 that there was 'increasing antipathy among the population of the north with regard to certain deeds perpetrated by the so-called Ovambo Home Guards'. The report described a particular incident, in which Home Guards had fired shots and burned down the house of a family in the north, after having chased the occupants from the property. The house belonged the the parents of Axel Johannes, a leading SWAPO official who had suffered years of detention and torture by the South African security police.[33]

Another local force feared and detested by the civilian population are the Special Constables, a paramilitary unit attached to the police. They have been used frequently to carry out attacks on workers' compounds. A number of brutal killings by Special Constables have come to light in recent years.

The existence of a special police counter-insurgency unit operating under the name Koevoet (crowbar) first came to light in May 1980, following the discovery of a death list naming a number of individuals to be assassinated by Koevoet. The unit, which was created in 1978 and consists of around 1,000 men, mostly Ovambos with white South African police commanders, has become notorious for atrocities and killings carried out among civilians in the north of the country.[34]

Other black Namibians have been involuntarily drawn into the militarisation process by a variety of pressures applied by the SADF and white Namibians. For example, black farmers wanting to settle on land abandoned by white farmers in the farming area around Outjo in central Namibia, have come under pressure from the area commander of Outjo's armed forces to join the security forces. Large areas of the 'white' farming region in central Namibia have been vacated by white farmers as PLAN combatants have made their presence felt in this part of the country. In 1981, 60 per cent. of farmhouses in the region around Tsumeb were reported to have been deserted.[35] This has created a 'security problem' for the SADF, which relies on the white population to report the presence of guerillas. Alarm systems, training camps and other security measures have been provided by the SADF to 'protect' the white population and at the same time encourage its cooperation. Black farmers wanting to participate in resettlement schemes introduced by the administration were told in 1981 that they 'had to give something in return'.[36]

Other black civilians, many of them young boys, have been drawn into the paramilitary structure through police recruitment campaigns. At a number of base camps established throughout the territory, they are trained in counter-insurgency techniques. A journalist who visited such camps in the Caprivi, Ovambo and Herero areas noted that there were 'an amazing number of youths, some not older than 12 years, who had been in the camp for more than two years'.[37] In Ovambo, several hundred people were being trained by the police. Training camps were also reported to exist in Kavango and Kaokoland. Most had apparently been established in 1979.[38] Brigadier Wandreg, second in command of the South African Police counter-insurgency unit, told journalists that the local population had been sceptical at first when the scheme was introduced, but that after enjoying some of the privileges going with the job, 'enthusiasm spread like wild fire'.[39]

There has been evidence, however, that in a number of cases people have been forced to join one of these units against their will and have fled at the first opportunity. One young Namibian described in an interview with SWAPO how, during a police raid on Katutura, the black township outside Windhoek, in September 1979, he was rounded up, together with hundreds of other residents. He said that he had been tortured and, in December 1979, had been taken to a place near Durban in South Africa with a group of 25 people. The group received intensive military training for about three months and was sent to the 'operational area' to fight disguised as SWAPO guerillas. When asked why he left this job, he said:'I did not look for that job and I was simply doing it at gunpoint while waiting for an appropriate chance to escape'.[40]

Resistance to being incorporated into the South African military machine surfaced strongly with the introduction of compulsory military service for all Namibians over the age of 16 in January 1981.

Protest rallies were organised throughout the territory to oppose the call-up and demand that conscription be abolished. In the recruitment drive, young men were reported to have been taken from the streets and sent for military service after only a few of those called up had reported for duty. Those making enquiries about their conscription were immediately enlisted. A marked military presence was reported in Windhoek to enforce the conscription law. Students and workers alike faced the threat of imminent recruitment. Schools were required to register boys due to reach the age of 16 during 1981.[41]

Large numbers of contract workers were reported in December 1980 to have left their workers' hostel in Katutura to return to their homes in the north of Namibia, out of fear of being conscripted. Men resident in the northern 'homelands' had been excluded from the draft, ostensibly on the grounds that the numbers called up would otherwise exceed demand. They were instead officially requested to volunteer with the tribal battalions already in existence in their respective areas.[42]

Police base for members of Koevoet, the Special Police counterinsurgency unit, in the Kaoko region.

Fenced in housing for blacks near Opuwo, Kaokoland.

Watchtower at South African military base, Ondangwa.

South African soldiers guarding military installations.

A unit of the South African Cape Corps, deployed in Namibia.

South African army trucks in northern Namibia.

Troops use dogs to attack demonstrators

Helicopters and helicopter gunships are used extensively.

A prisoner captured during a South African attack into Angola.

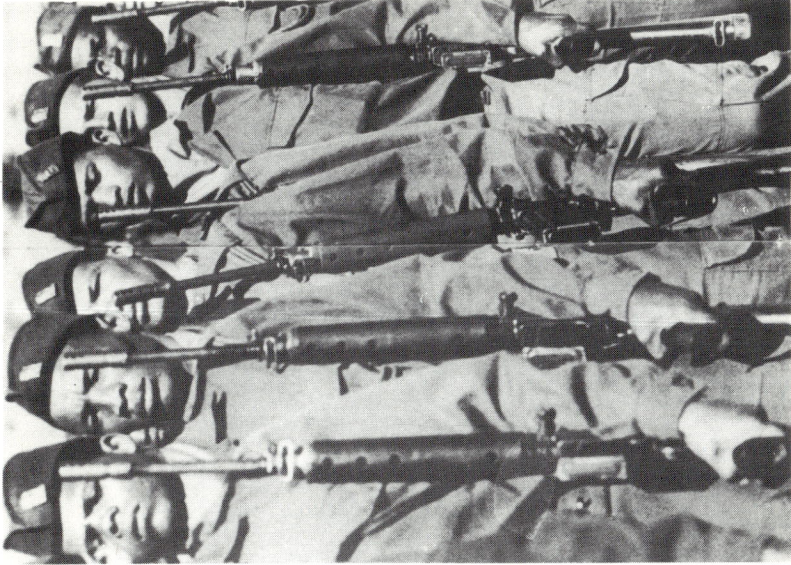

Members of the South West Africa Territory Force.

Victims of South Africa's aggression are used to frighten the local population.

South African troops are a familiar sight in the capital.

South African security forces are present at all SWAPO rallies. . . .

. . . .where they harrass and intimidate. . . .

SWAPO supporters.

The printing press of the Lutheran mission at Oniipa was blown up twice - in 1977 and 1980 - by South African forces.

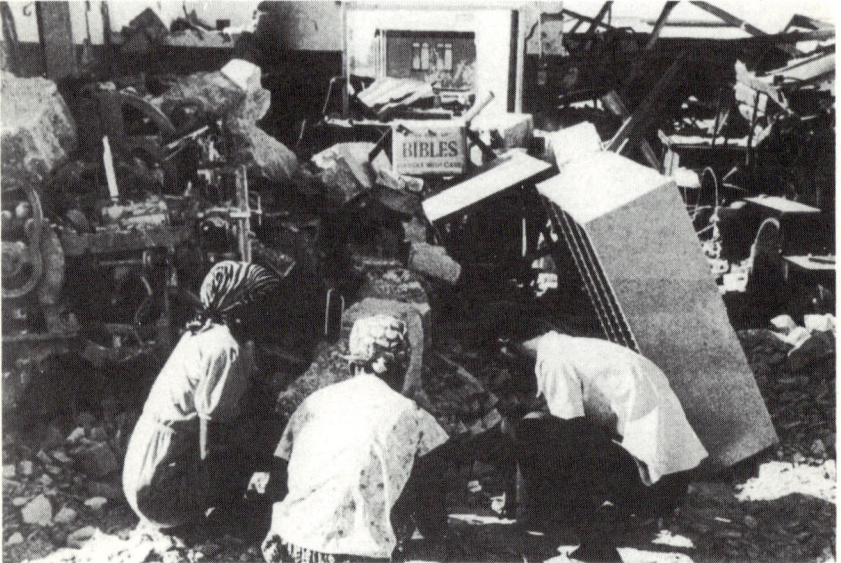

II THE MACHINERY OF REPRESSION

As the war in Namibia has intensified, a growing array of laws and regulations, designed to control every aspect of civilian life, has been imposed on the population. In its efforts to suppress support for SWAPO, the South African regime has attempted to cripple the liberation movement as a political force inside the country. Conscious of the widely held belief, both in Namibia and abroad, that SWAPO would overwhelmingly win genuinely free elections,[1] the South African security forces have resorted to mass arrests, detention without trial, torture and bannings of large numbers of SWAPO leaders and supporters, and have prevented the functioning of SWAPO's office in Windhoek by frequent raids and arrests of its workers. While the liberation movement is not officially banned, it has been virtually driven underground as a result of constant attacks on its members.

In addition, the regime has used emergency regulations, curfews, bans on public meetings and other measures to restrict all political activity opposed to its policies.

Mass Arrests

The entire leadership of SWAPO, as well as many SWAPO supporters, have been periodically arrested and detained for prolonged periods.

In August 1975, virtually all SWAPO leaders in Namibia were arrested and detained under the Terrorism Act and General Law Amendment Act. The arrests followed the assassination, by unknown assailants, of the Ovambo Chief Minister, Filemon Elifas.

In March/April 1978, virtually the entire leadership of SWAPO was again rounded up following the assassination of the Herero Chief, Clemens Kapuuo. Some were held until the end of October 1978.[2]

In December 1978, many arrests occurred during the run-up to the South African-organised 'internal' elections in the territory.[3]

In April 1979, over 50 top SWAPO officials were arrested and detained under Proclamation AG26, immediately prior to the announcement that a tribally-based National Assembly would be established. Some remained in detention for 15 months.[4]

Following the discovery by SWAPO of a death list in May 1980, naming more than 50 people whom the South African regime intended to kill, a number of people whose names were on the list were reported arrested or missing. A special police unit, operating under the name 'Koevoet', was apparently to carry out the assassinations.[5]

In 1980, the regime made increasing use of banning orders. SWAPO members released from detention were placed under restriction in their homes or areas where they resided, and prohibited from leaving that area, attending

17

meetings or receiving visitors.[6]

A Namibian lawyer, Lucia Hamutenya, gave a detailed account of the victimisation suffered by those arrested. As SWAPO's Secretary for Legal Affairs, she collected a wealth of evidence from former detainees, describing the severe torture, solitary confinement and overcrowding experienced by herself and other detainees.

She reported that:

> 'in the operational zone, torture has reached astronomical proportions. Thousands of people were rounded up in massive crackdowns carried out by South African soldiers between the months of June/July 1979. Suspected SWAPO supporters were picked up at their homes or arrested at roadblocks put up across the operational areas . . . Trenches have been used for detention purposes because of late regular prisons have been filled to capacity. Detainees held in these trenches have had their legs and hands tied behind their backs for 24 hours, and been subjected to torture'.

She described several specific cases of torture applied to individuals.[7]

By the early 1980s, open political activities by SWAPO inside the country had become virtually impossible. While the liberation movement has continued to organise public meetings, constant police harrassment and arrests have made these increasingly hazardous. A rally to celebrate Namibia Day on 26 August 1981, organised by SWAPO in Katutura, was dispersed by SA Police equipped with riot vehicles and thunderflashes, while plainclothes police were seen shooting a cine film of the proceedings.[8]

The Terrorism Act of 1967

Made retrospective to 1962 to allow for the trial of 37 SWAPO members, it provides for the death penalty for a wide definition of 'terroristic activities' such as 'intent to endanger the maintenance of law and order'. Empowers any high-ranking police officer to arrest any person suspected of being or having aided a 'terrorist' and provides for indefinite detention of people for interrogation.

The Combatting of Terrorism Bill

Debated in the National Assembly in December 1981, aimed to replace the Terrorism Act, sections of the General Law Amendment Act and the Internal Security Act of 1976.

Provisions: to abolish the death penalty, provide for a maximum sentence of 20 years imprisonment; could be imposed on any person convicted of informing or feeding guerilas.

As a result of strong opposition, particularly by Ovambo officials, the Bill was returned to a select committee of the National Assembly for review.

> ### The Riotous Assemblies Act 1956
> Extended to Namibia in 1976, it enables the South African government to ban any assembly or gathering which the police consider would constitute a threat to state security.
>
> ### The Suppression of Communism Act 1950
> Applied to Namibia in 1966, it empowers the South African State President to declare unlawful any organisation he believes to be connected in any way with, or pursuing the aims of, communism. In 1976, its name was changed to *Internal Security Act* and its scope broadened to provide for the detention of any individual suspected of endangering state security or the maintenance of public order, for three months incommunicado.
>
> (For a detailed survey of South African laws applied to Namibia, see *Laws Affecting Race Relations in South Africa,* South African Institute of Race Relations, 1978).

Emergency Regulations

Emergency measures, amounting to virtual martial law, have been in force in large areas of Namibia since 1972, when a state of emergency was declared in the Ovambo region to deal with the general strike of Namibian workers, led by Ovambo contract workers. Despite a total news ban imposed on the region at that time, reports filtered through of mass arrests and atrocities committed against civilians. Detainees were reported to be kept in steel-barred cages all over Ovambo, and a number of people were flogged in public.[9]

In 1976, a month after these emergency regulations were extended to Kavango and Caprivi, a major security sweep was carried out in secrecy by the South African army under the Codename 'Operation Cobra'. According to the testimony of a deserter from an SADF battalion involved in the operation, a total of 1,000 men were arrested by his battalion, including some boys aged 13. All the arrested men were tortured and taken to a detention camp.[10]

New emergency legislation was introduced in November 1977, replacing the earlier measures. This has been periodically amended to impose further restrictions on civilian life *(see boxes for details of various repressive laws)*. Reports document that these measures are applied systematically and that many civilians have found themselves questioned, detained and tortured by the security forces simply for being out of doors. A group of young Namibian refugees in Angola described their experiences in early 1981. They found that many of their normal activities were no longer possible because of the restrictions in force such as curfews, prohibitions on travel on certain roads or entry into certain areas. They could not go on excursions or camping because of the risk of being attacked by soldiers. People were no longer allowed to celebrate weddings because the security forces assumed that PLAN combatants were present at any large gathering. The local custom of helping each other in time of drought or shortages had been forced to stop because anyone found carrying food in large quantities was assumed to be taking it to PLAN fighters. In an interview published in *The Combatant*, the journal of PLAN (the People's Liberation Army of Namibia, SWAPO's military wing), it was explained:

> 'If one is meticulously dressed, then one is being identified with SWAPO soldiers. Also if one is not neatly dressed then the conclusion is that one is a SWAPO soldier. Likewise, if one is speaking faultless English one is called a SWAPO terrorist. Locally made boots, or those exported from South Africa, are sometimes mistaken for those of PLAN combatants. Many people have been tortured or detained because of the shoes they wore. In the war zone one must not visit a friend because it is seen as a mission to contact SWAPO combatants.'[11]

As a result of the dusk to dawn curfew in force in most of the north, local trade has been disrupted as markets have had to close early. In Ovambo, an amendment to the security regulations in February 1980 expressly prohibited anyone from selling goods between sunset and sunrise.[12]

Proclamation AG9 (Security Districts Proclamation), promulgated on 11 November 1977. Applied to Ovambo, Kavango and Eastern Caprivi. Provides for:

* restrictions on residence and movement of persons in a security district

* any area situated next to a security district and along an international boundary to be declared a prohibited area, forbidding people to enter or be in that area

* search, seizure, arrest and detention for 72 hours without a warrant.

* access to a legal advisor only with the approval of the Administrator General

---

AG9 has been amended a number of times:

13 June 1978   *Proclamation AG34* (Security Districts Amendment) Makes it illegal for any person to drive or travel in a vehicle or to pick up a passenger during the night without written consent from an Officer of the Peace or an Officer of the security forces.

10 May 1979	Regulations contained in AG9 were extended southwards to include the magisterial districts of Windhoek, Tsumeb, Outjo, Okahandja, Otjiwarongo and Grootfontein. The period allowed for detention was extended to 30 days.
28 June 1979	AG9 was amended to ban all movement at night in Ovambo. Provisions forbidding the movement of all motor vehicles at night were extended to cover bicycles and pedestrians. Penalty: three years imprisonment and/or a R600 fine.
19 December 1979	*Proclamation AG114* Certain sections of AG9 were extended to Kaokoland, including the control of residence, movement and activity of any person living in a security district, the power to designate an area a 'prohibited area', powers of arrest, detention and search without a warrant, and 24 hours notice of all meetings.
6 February 1980	AG9 was amended to empower the security forces to prohibit travel on any road in Ovambo at times they might specify. Prohibited any person selling merchandise from one half hour after sunset to one half hour before sunrise in Ovambo without the consent of the authorites.
13 October 1980	*Proclamation AG161* Requires any person in a security district who gives medical assistance to persons wounded or injured in suspicious circumstances to report the matter without delay to the security forces.

Detention Laws

In addition to these regulations, a number of other laws allow for the arbitrary arrest and detention of anyone suspected of supporting SWAPO *(see boxes)*. While these are widely and systematically used, there are also many reported cases of people being arbitrarily arrested, detained and tortured for a few days, and then released, without ever being told under which law they are being held. Numerous reports suggest that there is a deliberate policy of intimidation and terror applied to all civilians in the north of the country. In addition, indiscipline among the police and army has led to widespread acts of brutality, including massacres of whole villages *(see Chapter V)*.

Under these circumstances, civilians supporting SWAPO are under constant threat of victimisation. A new law, the *Combatting of Terrorism Bill,* which was debated in the Namibian National Assembly in late 1981, contained provisions for a 20 year sentence to be imposed on anyone aiding SWAPO guerillas. This meant that anyone giving food or shelter to SWAPO guerillas, or being suspected of doing so, could be given the maximum sentence. The Bill, which was intended to replace the Terrorism Act of 1962, a South African law applied to Namibia, was strongly opposed by Ovambo officials, including those who normally align themselves with the South African-sponsored internal regime. They argued that the Ovambo people were already bearing the brunt of the war. As a result, the Bill was transferred to a committee to investigate its implications. It had not been referred back to the National Assembly by the autumn of 1982.

Proclamation AG26, April 1978

Provision for the detention of persons to prevent political violence and intimidation.

Provides for the detention without trial for an unlimited period of any person believed to 'promote violence and intimidation'. No visits from relations or lawyers are permitted, and detainees can be held at any place designated by the Administrator General and moved at any time. Detention under AG26 cannot be challenged in court.

Other Security Measures

A number of other measures have from time to time been announced, giving an indication of the regime's growing concern over the success of guerilla activities. They have allowed tighter control by the security forces over civilian movement, as well as giving security assistance to sympathisers of the regime.

White-owned farms have been singled out for protection because of the large numbers which have been abandoned by their owners.[13] In May 1979, 40 farms in the northern cattle ranching area were given military protection. Two South African soldiers were posted to each farm and instructed to accompany the farmers and their families wherever they went.[14] In November 1979, a priority area of 888 farms was identified which would receive interest-free loans to establish radio alarm systems and security fences.[15]

A convoy system with armed escorts was introduced in September 1979 on the 130 km stretch of major road between Ondangwa and Oshivelo,[16] and in January 1980, the training of special police was intensified so they could provide more effective protection to tribal leaders sympathetic to South Africa. Military escorts were also introduced on a stretch of road in Kaokoland in February 1980.[17] In Ovambo, security forces provide armed escorts for government inoculation teams, officials who travel to pay pensions, inspectors of schools and building projects of the local (bantustan) government.[18]

The Aviation Act was amended by *Proclamation AG66* of 16 July 1979 to prohibit any civilian aircraft from flying in a restricted area between 6 p.m. and 6 a.m. and requiring pilots to file a flight plan and obtain specific permission. Aircraft were prohibited from flying below 3,000 feet.[19]

In April 1981, a ban was imposed on all movement between dusk and dawn in south west Kavango on the grounds that civilian movement hindered the security forces.[20]

New legislation giving the security forces and local magistrates wide powers to prohibit meetings was passed by the National Assembly in December 1981.[21]

Prohibition and Notification of Meetings Act No. 22 of 1981 (23 December 1981)

Gives wide power to the security forces and local magistrates to prohibit meetings. Requires notification of any meeting of more than 20 persons to the local magistrate, including submission of information about time and place of meeting, names of organisation and speakers and, if required by the magistrate, of the constitution of the organisation holding the meeting. Empowers the magistrate to ban any meeting if he considers that it advocates the overthrow of the existing order. Provides for three years imprisonment or a maximum fine of R300 or both.

Civilian Resistance

The widespread repression suffered by the Namibian population at the hands of the South African and indigenous security forces appears to have had little success in reducing the level of support for SWAPO, but instead to have strengthened hostility towards South Africa's presence.

An incident recorded by a foreign journalist visiting Namibia in January 1981 illustrates the effect that army brutality has had on people. During a three hour raid by South African security forces in an unspecified location, all black males were marched one by one to an army ambulance marked with a Red Cross to be screened by a hooded informer. Afterwards, they were lined up in a field, where the security forces fired guns over their heads and made them shout in unison 'We hate SWAPO. We don't hate whites'. One black person from Ovambo commented to the journalist: 'If you were not a SWAPO (supporter) before that, you were afterwards'.[22]

A church delegation visiting Namibia on behalf of the South African Council of Churches in February 1982, found that all church leaders they had spoken to with the exception of one, expressed the view that the majority of people in the country supported SWAPO, while there was growing resentment over the continued presence of the South African army. 'The longer the South African military stays in the territory, the larger grows the support for SWAPO', one of the delegates said.[23]

Civilians protect and shelter PLAN fighters under the very eyes of the South African armed forces, enabling the guerillas to merge with the local population while preparing sabotage actions. When SWAPO guerillas attacked the large military base at Oshakati in January 1981 using heavy rockets of 122 mm calibre, no traces could be found of the attackers. As the *Windhoek Observer* pointed out, this raised the question of how a number of heavy rockets could have been transported without detection by the South African army. While the security forces claimed that the guerillas had returned to Angola the same night, SWAPO pointed out that it would be impossible to cover a distance of 100 km to and fro under these circumstances, and stressed that 'the combatants of PLAN are operating from within Namibia'. When guerillas destroyed part of a telephone line between Ondangwa and Oshakati, only 400 metres from the South African air base and army camp at Ondangwa, the same newspaper noted: 'Guerillas are walking around at night, passing the (Ondangwa) airbase at 200 metres. Many find their way into town dressed as civilians to carry out reconnoitring, and to gain intelligence, especially on the movements of army equipment and personnel'.[24]

Calls by the South African army for witnesses of SWAPO sabotage actions reportedly meet with passive resistance. Local residents claimed they had heard nothing after a PLAN unit had blown up a bridge on a main road in April 1981. A reporter interviewing local residents about the incident found that 'everywhere the answer was the same, they had not heard or seen a thing. . . although the explosion must have been earsplitting to cause the bridge to collapse in its entirety'.[25]

In addition to sheltering and feeding SWAPO guerillas, civilians also play a more active role in providing information on army installations or accompanying guerillas on their missions. During an attack on a police station at Nkurenkuru in Kavango in May 1982, civilians were reported to have been with the group of guerillas. According to newspaper reports, local residents led SWAPO guerillas to a spot practically inside the police camp. One reporter commented: 'The security forces would like to think that the assistance given by the population to the guerillas is under duress, but speaking to the police, soldiers and members of the population, a different picture emerges'.[26]

Where possible, civilians protect themselves and others from army violence by refusing to inform and by warning neighbours of dangers. In Ovambo, a visitor found that local people placed branches over mines planted by the South Africans to warn others.[27] When offered a 'tip' to give information, they remain silent. One journalist found that people had come to dread offers of money for giving information, not knowing any longer to whom they were talking.[28]

24

III THE CHURCHES SPEAK OUT

The churches in Namibia, representing approximately 90 per cent of the population, are uniquely placed to witness the plight of their parishioners. Since 1971, when the Lutheran churches addressed an Open Letter to the South African Prime Minister condemning the suffering inflicted on the Namibian people, church leaders have increasingly voiced their protest against South Africa's military occupation of the country. Namibian church representatives have often been instrumental in exposing brutalities and injustices committed by the security forces. They have increasingly been supported by international church bodies who have sent delegations to visit Namibia. Church support for Namibian refugees, and appeals by churches of all denominations for support of the Namibian people's struggle for independence, have grown over the years.

As a consequence of their open condemnation of South African violence against the Namibian people, the churches have themselves frequently been the victims of harassment. Foreign missionaries have been expelled, church property destroyed and services broken up by security forces.

Church Statements

In February 1982, a press statement issued by Namibia's largest church, the Evangelical Lutheran Ovambokavango Church (ELOC) described the sufferings experienced by the people in Ovambo. In the past few years, the statement said, 'suffering and torture were predominant, even more than at any other time in the past'. Hundreds of the church's parishioners had lost their lives. Private houses had been set on fire and many innocent civilians had their properties either destroyed or were robbed of them. Hundreds of people, both male and female, had been held in jails. In some cases their whereabouts were still unknown. Young men were forced to undergo military training, against their will. There were waves of persecution and torture which had caused thousands of church members and other members of the Namibian nation to become exiles. Some pastors and lay preachers had been imprisoned at one time or another. ELOC added that at the time of its Synod held in December 1981, 13 percent of the 300 delegates had personal experience of being jailed and tortured. It appealed for the people to be given a chance, without delay, to elect their own leaders through the implementation of the United Nations Plan for Namibian independence.[1]

Similar statements, often giving detailed evidence of atrocities committed against members of their congregations, have come from other individual churches and from the Council of Churches in Namibia (CCN), an umbrella body which groups togther the six main churches, including the Anglican, Catholic and Episcopal churches.

In a document presented to the South African Prime Minister during his visit to Namibia in February 1982, the CCN recalled its longstanding concern about violation of human rights in the country. Since then the situation had grown much worse. 'We know of the killing of innocent people, of the wanton destruction of property and of beatings, detention, solitary confinement and torture of the local population', the statement said. The curfew in force in the north prevented people from being taken to hopital if they fell ill or were burned or injured during the night. Local people were distressed at seeing army recruits teaching in their schools or working in their hospitals.[2]

Foreign Church Visits

A number of representatives from international church bodies have visited Namibia to carry out their own investigations. They have experienced at first hand the effects of the war and have added their voices in protest.

The British Council of Churches, which sent a delegation to Namibia in November 1981, stated in its subsequent report that while SWAPO guerillas were regarded by the civilian population as 'children of the people', the security forces maintained a reign of arbitrary terror against which people felt they had no redress. The church delegates collected details of twenty individual cases of atrocities suffered by civilians at the hands of the security forces; most of these had taken place in the six weeks preceding the team's arrival. In one instance, they met a woman whose home had been the target of more than 1,500 bullets, allegedly fired to 'protect' her from non-existent guerillas. Her two boys of eight and fifteen years were killed. The cartridges were counted by independent witnesses.

The report described as a particularly objectionable practice the security forces' habit of dragging through the villages behind their vehicles the corpses of those killed, whom they alleged to be 'terrorists'. The bodies of the young men were exhibited to their parents, to villagers, and even to young children in school. This desecration of the dead had proved totally counterproductive and caused deep resentment among the people, according to the delegation.[3]

In May 1982, the Southern African Catholic Bishop's Conference issued a damning report on the behaviour of the security forces, after church representatives had visited Namibia. They interviewed 180 people during their investigations, and heard accounts of detention and torture.

One man described how he was hung by the neck with just his feet touching the ground, and then subjected to electric shock treatment before being thrown blindfolded into a lake. A woman told how during her detention she was constantly beaten up and given electric shocks while chained hand and foot to a chair. During shock treatment she was gagged, a cloth soaked in salt water being placed across her open mouth and tied tightly at the back of her neck. The shock treatment caused haemorrhages and affected her kidneys. She had to undergo an operation in hospital, and was then returned to gaol. The gaol was an iron shack — hot and dirty. The wound from the operation festered.

The report cited several other cases of torture. People also described how South African soldiers 'break into homes, beat up residents, shoot people, steal and kill cattle and often pillage stores and tea rooms'. The delegation heard that women were often raped. 'It is not unknown for a detachment to break into a house and while black soldiers keep watch over the family, white soldiers select the best-looking girls and take them into the veld to rape them', the report said. The South African troops were known as 'bloodsuckers' by the local inhabitants.

That detention and interrogation in any part of the country are accompanied by beating, torture, spare diet and solitary confinement is accepted as common knowledge. 'We found this attitude among most church representatives we met and among many others as well' the delegation noted. It found that 'support for SWAPO is massive' and that 'it would easily be victorious in any free and fair elections held under United Nations supervision'. The church representatives were told that it was not SWAPO's policy to intimidate, because as a guerilla army it was dependent on the goodwill of the people. People did not fear SWAPO guerillas but the South African security forces, which were known throughout Namibia as an 'army of occupation'.

The report concluded that there was a universal consensus, with South Africa virtually the only dissenting voice, that South Africa had no right to be in Namibia. The great majority of Namibians had one overriding desire and that was the implementation of UN Security Council Resolution 435, resulting in a ceasefire, the withdrawal of South African security forces, and the holding of elections under United Nations auspices.[4]

Attacks on Churches

As the war in Namibia has intensified, the churches have found their work increasingly difficult. Traditionally they have provided some of the few opportunities for education, health care and community services, particularly in remote areas. However, the imposition of curfews, the expulsion of foreign church workers, arrests of local clergy and fire-bomb attacks on church institutions have greatly reduced this work.

In a letter to the South African Prime Minister in February 1982, the CCN drew attention to these developments. It reminded the Prime Minister of the Open Letter published by the Namibian churches in 1971, in which they expressed their concern about violations of human rights in the country. Since then, they had experienced

> 'the deportation of leaders and workers; some were refused visas, others with permanent residence status had their permits withdrawn, some were arrested and detained, all without recourse to a court of law'.[5]

The Lutheran and Anglican churches have been subjected to a number of violent attacks on their property and their workers. The ELOC printing press in Oniipa was blown up twice by bomb blasts, one in 1973 and again in 1980. The editor of the church newspaper, *Omukwetu,* was forced to flee into exile after publishing details about a death squad called Koevoet operating as part of the security forces in the north.[6]

St. Mary's Anglican Mission at Odibo has been periodically raided by police, its archdeacon arrested and its workers beaten up by the police. In July 1976, about 150 security force members raided the mission and detained the archdeacon, Rev. Shilongo, for two days. Three weeks previously, his private secretary and her fiancé had been assaulted by tribal police. The fiancé, Thorothimus Jacobus, later died of his injuries.[7]

St. Mary's Mission was again raided by South African troops in August 1979, and Rev. Shilongo arrested. During another raid in July 1980, police reportedly took mission property, broke down doors in a workshop, the hospital and girls' hostel.[8] In June 1981, the seminary attached to the mission was completely destroyed by a bomb. Because of the curfew, residents of the mission were unable to look for any culprits.[9]

Church services at two parishes in the north of Namibia were brutally broken up by South African soldiers in May 1982. At Elombe, a Sunday worship service attended by between 600 and 700 people came to an abrupt halt when two army trucks arrived and soldiers surrounded the church building. Bishop Dumeni, head of ELOC who was visiting the parish for a thanksgiving ceremony, reported how his attempts to be allowed to continue the service were countered by the army commander with insults and the threat: 'I can shoot all these people'. The congregation was ordered to leave the church, with threats of being shot if they refused. All the men were interrogated and beaten. Some were so badly hurt that they were unable to continue with the service when the soldiers left an hour later. At Onayena, some 15 km away, a similar incident took place on the same day; two civilians were reportedly beaten so badly that they had to be taken to hospital.[10] Protests by Bishop Dumeni and by the Lutheran World Federation to the South African Prime Minister about the incident, as well as the allegations of army brutality made by many other organisations, resulted in the setting up of a Commission of Inquiry by the Ovambo tribal government and by the South African Minister of Defence. The SADF announced that one soldier had been court martialled and that others would probably also be prosecuted in connection with the incident at Elombe.[11] Doubts have been expressed, however, both by the churches and others, about the value of such commissions which involve the army investigating itself.[12]

Church Work Curtailed

To reduce the voices of protest from churches, the South African authorities have expelled a large number of missionaries and church workers over the years. Most prominent among them have been Bishop Colin Winter, Anglican

Bishop of Damaraland, who was expelled in 1972; his successor Bishop Wood, expelled in 1975; and Father Heinz Hunke, who published detailed evidence of torture and assault on detainees by the South African security police and army, deported in July 1978.[13] Finnish missionaries, who have worked in Namibia for many years, have been refused extensions of their residence permits. As a result, their number has steadily declined.

The debilitating effect on the churches' work of South Africa's military occupation was described by the Bishop of ELOC, Kleopas Dumeni:

'The work of the church is very much affected by the bush war in the country. Because roads are being mined, we cannot visit our parishes and congregations to the extent that we would like. . .

We are kept awake at night by the sound of arms and the heavy bursts and explosion of heavy guns and cannons as well as the ceaseless droning of armed vehicles and planes alike. The all-night curfew has recently been extended to the Okavango area too—covering in that way the whole length and breadth of ELOC's terrain of activities and ministry'.[15]

His statement was echoed by the Anglican Bishop, James Kauluma, who stressed that the war had hampered the growth of the Anglican Church in many ways. As a result of the creation of a free-fire zone by the South African army between southern Angola and northern Namibia, the church had been forced to close down clinics, hospitals and schools. These were indispensable amenities for rural communities, he said. The Holy Cross Mission in the east had to close down completely. St. Mary's Mission had also to close down a school in Odibo. 'Our church has lost many followers through the war situation. Worshippers who usually come to our border churches from southern Angola for fellowship have been cut off from us completely', he said.[16]

IV SOUTH AFRICA'S DESTRUCTION OF THE SOCIAL INFRASTRUCTURE

The War Enters Schools

Young black people in Namibia have grown up surrounded by the institutions of apartheid, reinforced by military and police violence. As in South Africa, young Namibians have played an important part in fighting for the liberation of their country. Their experiences at school have often been instrumental in making them aware of the racially discriminatory, repressive system they are forced to live under. The system of Bantu Education, the presence of armed South African soldiers in their schools and, since late 1980, the threat of conscription into the armed forces, have all contributed towards young people's rejection of South Africa's occupation of Namibia. Many began to attend SWAPO meetings while at school, and experienced police brutality at these meetings. They found that identification with SWAPO tended to lead to expulsion from school, and since the 1970s many have crossed the border into Angola or Zambia.

Student Protests

Student protests against Bantu Education, which was offically extended to Namibia in 1970, have usually embraced a deeper protest against the whole South African system of repression, exemplified by the presence of military and paramilitary forces in schools. In the mid-1970s there were a number of student protests resulting in expulsions and arrests. As news of the Soweto uprising in South Africa during the summer of 1976 reached Namibia, black students throughout the territory were inspired by these events. They boycotted examinations held under the terms of the Bantu Education Act. Leaflets attacking Bantu Education as the 'instrument of the homelands policy' were circulated. At one school in Damaraland, police were reported to have baton-charged a protest meeting, and armoured cars to have been called in.[1] In the aftermath of these events, many students fled the country, while inside Namibia a number were arrested.[2] Two presented statements in court claiming that they had been tortured.[3]

In July 1977, students were expelled from several schools for their political beliefs. 17 students were expelled from Okarara Teacher Training college and secondary school in November 1977, and a further 90 students were expelled from Ongwediva High School after attending a SWAPO meeting on 9 October 1977.

One Namibian, who left his country in 1980 after spending several periods in detention, explained:

> 'Politics could not be mentioned (at school), if you were a SWAPO as I was. Although most of our teachers were white,

some were black, and some were paid informers. . . After the riots of 1976, thirty or so students were arrested. Some were released and came back to school with swollen faces, as a warning to the rest of us I suppose. About six were brought to trial. But after the riots, until the end of my schooling, we had white teachers in soldiers' uniforms carrying guns even in lessons'.[4]

That school students were actively supporting SWAPO's armed struggle was admitted by the South African security forces in 1982. During a major offensive by PLAN guerillas in Namibia in May 1982, it became clear that civilians, including school students, had led the guerillas to their targets. A pupil from the Kandjimi Murenga Secondary School in the Kavango area was arrested after an attack on the residence of South African soldiers serving as teachers at the school. One soldier was killed. The school student was reported to have woken the soldiers asking for medical treatment. As the lights went on, handgrenades were thrown through the windows. Among the tracks found around the school were those of three or four civilians.[5]

Lessons at Gunpoint

The presence of white South African soldiers as teachers in Namibian schools is part of South Africa's policy of 'winning the hearts and minds of the people' *(see Chapter VI)*. To Namibian students, they represent the hated apartheid system reinforced by the gun. A Namibian woman, describing her experiences at school, stressed that the South African soldiers teaching her all carried guns.

'Imagine somebody teaching you, and if you make a mistake, or if he suspects you, he would just point his gun at you, telling you that he would shoot you or your mother'.

In the hostel where she lived, soldiers guarded the main entrance.[6]

Police and army interference in schools has been reported on a number of occasions. In one case personnel at a school lodged an objection about interference by the security police who were trying to bribe pupils to spy on other pupils and teachers.[7] Children who had fled to Angola told a SWAPO medical officer that South African troops had visited their schools.[8] Some 40 members of the Ovambo Home Guard were reported to have attacked and harassed students at the Oshakati Secondary School in northern Namibia in January 1980, injuring two students. In a letter to a local church newspaper, *Omukwetu*, an eye-witness said: 'It was reminiscent of Kassinga and Soweto when the soldiers continuously and mercilessly attacked us'.[9]

Closures and Shortages

The escalation of the war has disrupted the already inferior and inadequate education system further. Existing shortages in school buildings, teachers and materials have been exacerbated by the closure of schools in the north as a consequence of South Africa's military activities, and building programmes for new schools have been affected. In the Ovambo region, a shortage of 2,600 classrooms was reported in October 1980. R30 million were needed for the construction of new schools, and R50 million for school hostels.[10] According to official government statistics, six schools were forced to close in the Ovambo region during 1979/80,[11] though the number was put at 15 by a member of the tribal internal party, the Democratic Turnhalle Alliance (DTA), who said that approximately 20,000 children were affected.[12] In June 1981, a South African civil servant in Namibia stated that 19 of Ovambo's 450 schools were closed.[13] This was despite the use of SADF personnel to fill posts vacated by civilian teachers.

Militarisation in Schools

With the introduction of compulsory military service for all male youths between the age of 16 and 25 in January 1981, students have become one of the prime targets for recruitment. In October 1980, the Department of Education sent circulars to all schools instructing principals to register all boys due to reach the age of 16 by 1981.[14] As conscription proceeded in 1981, reports indicated a growing militarisation of schools, forcing students to either respond to the call-up or flee from their country.

It was reported in 1981 that boarding schools were being constructed at South African military bases to accommodate school students and thereby prevent them from evading conscription and/or leaving the country to join SWAPO. According to *The Combatant,* the journal of SWAPO's armed wing, the South African army's intention was to train such students so that they could be used as a 'shield' in the event of guerilla attacks on military bases, thereby creating 'favourable conditions for accusing SWAPO of killing civilians'.[15]

The Coloured tribal authorities announced in early 1981 that pupils at Coloured secondary schools throughout the country would be trained as school cadets. They would be issued with uniforms and would undergo instructions under the SWA Territory Force (SWATF). A training camp would be established and teachers trained to take over the instruction of cadets. The programme would facilitate greater understanding of the functions of the SWATF, an official of the Coloured tribal authority said.[16]

To call-up has driven thousands of young Namibians into exile. Unable to obtain a good education in Namibia, and faced with the prospect of having to fight against their comrades in SWAPO's military wing, they have increasingly joined the liberation movement. By February 1981, some 5,000 were reported to have fled across the border to Angola.[17] Frequent claims by the South African authorities that SWAPO guerillas have 'abducted' schoolchildren by forcibly transporting them across the border to Angola are contradicted by statements from pupils themselves. For example, a statement by a Catholic priest refuted claims by the South African government that a group of pupils had been abducted in early 1982. He said he had received letters from some of the pupils stating that they had arranged to be fetched by SWAPO guerillas from their school in Ovambo.[18]

Many students have joined the growing protest movement inside Namibia, calling for an end to conscription and South Africa's illegal occupation.[19] Those who identified themselves as SWAPO supporters during their initial training period found themselves victimised by the military authorities. A group of trainees at the Okahandja Military Training school who declared their SWAPO sympathies were reportedly disarmed, suspended from training school and sent to the operational area for 'reorientation'.[20]

Victimisation of Teachers

Teachers have increasingly seen their schools taken over by South African soldiers placed there to promote the idea of the army as a social benefactor and to act as informers. Those teachers known to oppose Bantu Education, or suspected of having SWAPO affiliations, have faced arrest, detention and dismissal from their jobs. A number of such cases have been documented in recent years.

In September 1973, a memorandum produced in Ovambo by unknown sources and published in the South African press, reported that

> 'teachers have been arrested at schools in the presence of the pupils and classes closed. The Ovambo authorities have discussed the "competence" of Ovambo teachers to teach the youth. SWAPO-minded teachers are not "fit to teach" and 30 of such teachers have already been removed from their posts'.[21]

One particular incident at a primary school in Ongwediva was described by a Namibian school teacher in a letter to the President of the United Nations Council for Namibia in October 1974. Ms. Nahambo Shamena, who had fled from Namibia in July that year, gave an account of the arrest of a teacher at the school in 1973, and the subsequent arrest of the headmaster. Valde Namunya, the teacher, was arrested by South African police after having spoken at a SWAPO rally. He had condemned the South African policy of Bantu Education as oppressive. His pupils, aged from seven to 15, tried to prevent his arrest and the police had to call in reinforcements. 'Every member of the troop had his gun pointed at the children, waiting for the command to shoot if necessary', Ms. Shamena wrote. Shortley after that incident, police returned to arrest the headmaster, Shoombe. Again the children tried to prevent the arrest, using sticks and stones and grabbing Shombe. The police responded by mercilessly batoning the children.[22]

As educators, teachers are uniquely placed to promote political awareness among pupils and students, and as a result those suspected of SWAPO sympathies have become the target of repressive laws. Legislation providing for the dismissal of teachers or civil servants from their jobs for political reasons was introduced by the Ovambo tribal authorities in 1980. Anyone employed in such a position and reported to the security forces for holding political views opposing South African policies could be detained and would automatically lose his or her job.[23]

Health Under Attack

The health service in Namibia is inextricably linked to the apartheid system imposed by South Africa. Health care is organised along racially segregated lines, with services for the black majority rudimentary and in many areas virtually non-existent. As a result of the war, services have further deteriorated, clinics have been closed and medical personnel become more scarce. This was confirmed by a member of the DTA who admitted that in the Ovambo region, there was virtually no medical assistance available due to the war. Clinics had been burnt down, and local people had to walk up to 50 kilometres in some cases if they needed medical attention.[24] Endemic diseases, such as the plague, have reappeared, and others, such as malaria, have become more widespread due to the absence of immunisation programmes.

Existing community health services and mission hospitals have been crippled by the effect of South Africa's military operations. Security legislation has restricted the ability of health workers to give treatment, and patients have stayed away from hospitals for fear of harassment by the police or army. Doctors and nurses have in some cases been attacked, detained and tortured for alleged collaboration with SWAPO, and hospitals have been subjected to police raids.

South Africa has used the shortage of skilled medical personnel to place national servicemen into health centres, making the population in the north virtually completely dependent on the security forces for medical treatment.

The government of a future independent Namibia will, no doubt, be faced with a legacy of ill-health prevalent among the population, exacerbated by the effects of the war. The number of war-wounded or disabled is unknown, as is the number of people suffering mental ill-health as a result of their war experiences. Those who reach the refugee settlements in neighbouring Angola are given treatment by SWAPO medical personnel, and are rehabilitated into the community through productive work and crafts. According to SWAPO's Secretary for Health and Social Affairs, many of the refugees arrive with tuberculosis, typhoid or other diseases, and need treatment. SWAPO has a rehabilitation programme for war victims, and is training nurses, doctors and midwives. In the refugee settlements, people are receiving for the first time, the health care they have been deprived of in their country.

Services Crippled by the War

The imposition of curfews, legislation restricting doctors and nurses in their tasks of providing medical assistance, and the hazards of travelling in an area swarming with soldiers and police, have led to the breakdown of community health care. People in Ovambo used to gather daily at clinics which served as community health centres, but now they are increasingly frightened to move about, according to a Namibian nursing administrator.[25] A Finnish missionary in the area stressed in 1980 that the all-night curfew in force in Ovambo made it difficult for missionaries to administer medical attention at night.[26] An amendment to the Security Districts Proclamation AG9 *(see Chapter II)* was passed in 1981 requiring any person in a Security District who gave medical assistance to report the matter without delay to the security forces.[27]

The difficult conditions resulting from the war were explained by a matron in charge of the hospital at Opuwo in the Kaoko region. There was a severe shortage of trained personnel, and consequently half the hospital could not be used. A plan to train health workers who could treat common illnesses in outlying areas had to be abandoned because of the war. 'You can't post people out like that with the war situation being what it is', the matron said. Travel was a major problem, and food for the hospital had to be fetched every week from Okahandja, a town north of Windhoek, by truck. A refrigerated truck, which used to supply the food regularly, no longer did so because the driver refused to travel on the roads because of the war.[28]

Increase in Disease

Infectious diseases, such as malaria and typhoid, have increased as immunisation programmes have had to be abandoned. Although statistics are generally not available, reports from medical personnel working in the north of the country and from officials generally concerned with health questions, indicate that this has reached serious proportions. The matron at Opuwo hospital, for instance, stressed that malaria and gastroenteritis were endemic in the Kaoko area. A malaria epidemic was reported in 1982, but an even more serious one was expected the following year. One of the main reasons cited by an official was the war, which had restricted programmes to eliminate the malaria-bearing mosquito to one-fifth of the infected area. There was a real danger that malaria-bearing larvae could mature, thus increasing the risks. Another official called the situation alarming, but said 'there is little we can do with the war as it is in the north'. He confirmed that the incidence of malaria was also on the increase in the south of the country. Because the war had considerably restricted the movement of health officers in the north, many malaria sufferers could only be treated in the main centres. Medical teams were travelling with military protection; many people were scared to come forward for treatment.[29] Two church-run hospitals in Ovambo had seen more than 3,000 cases between them over a period of two weeks in mid-1982, according to one report.[30]

Other diseases such as polio, diphtheria and the plague are also reported to be prevalent in the north of the country. Children died each year of diphtheria because they had not been immunised, a nursing administrator said, and the plague occurred in part of Ovambo during August and September.[31]

Army Interference

Many health posts in the north are run entirely by South African soldiers. This is in line with South Africa's policy, practised in other spheres such as education, agriculture, etc., aimed at presenting the armed forces in a humane light *(see Chapter VI)* The state hospital in Opuwo, for instance, has no civilian doctors and relies entirely on national servicemen. An army medical orderly fills the post of pharmacist.[32] According to a report published in the journal of the SADF in 1978, 'hundreds of South African medics do national military service (in Namibia) and also train the local population in para-medical techniques'.[33]

The army appears to have been almost completely unsuccessful in improving its image through 'civic action' and in fact to have created much resentment. According to one white nurse, 'the doctors in uniform are not welcomed by most Ovambos'.[34]

Violence Against Health Personnel

Civilian institutions and organisations providing social services to the Namibian population are inevitably drawn into the violent conflict. Those suspected of providing any kind of support to SWAPO find themselves victims of army and police attacks. There have been a number of reports of raids by the South African security forces on hospitals, and of arrests of medical personnel. For instance, the superintendent of the Lutheran Hospital at Onandjokwe, Dr. Nafta Hamata, was arrested at the hospital in 1980 and detained in solitary confinement in Windhoek for two months. During his detention, he suffered maltreatment and was reported to have been deprived of basic facilities.[35]

The Lutheran Nakayale Hospital at Ondangwa was subjected to repeated harassment by the army during late 1980, and a Finnish nurse at the hospital was accused of being implicated in the assassination of a patient who was a member of the Ovambo tribal government. The hospital was raided by an army unit on 21 October, and several other incidents of harassment and gunfire around the hospital compound were reported. The nurse, Kaino Kovanen, was threatened with expulsion after the shooting of a patient ten days after the army raid. Rejection of the charge by the head of the Lutheran church in Ovambo, Bishop Dumeni, led to an investigation by the authorities who completely cleared Ms. Kovanen of all charges.[36]

Another church hospital, at St. Mary's Mission in Odibo, was vandalised by South African police during a raid on the mission in July 1980. Bishop Kauluma, the head of the Anglican church in Namibia, described the behaviour of the police and the extensive damage done to the mission's property in a subsequent report. A large number of South African police, both black and white, entered the mission buildings and, without speaking to any of the residents, began taking property from different areas of the mission. They took doors from the hospital building and the nurses' quarters and broke other doors and windows; sheets of corrugated iron, which were used for some hospital shelters, were also removed. Similar damage was done to other buildings such as the workshop area, a girls' hostel, offices and the church building itself, and a large number of items were taken. Bishop Kauluma added that 'this is not the first time that the police from Ohangwena have come to take mission property'. He recalled a similar incident in November 1979.[37]

The more recent police action was carried out while the head of St. Mary's Mission, Archdeacon Shilongo, was being kept in detention.[38]

A student nurse who had worked at the Oshakati state hospital described her experience of army behaviour, after she had fled to Angola. According to her statement, South African soldiers planted landmines and explosives in the hospital compound and then blamed SWAPO. In one incident, an elderly hospital worker watched South African soldiers plant an anti-truck mine on the road near the entrance to the hospital. A driver who was to take the nurses from their living quarters to the hospital was instructed by the army to follow the same road. He was warned by the elderly worker, who was subsequently arrested by the army and was not heard of again.[39]

Another nurse working at the same hospital between 1975 and 1977, who was later one of those captured during South Africa's attack on the Kassinga refugee settlement in Angola, described the work she was involved in at the hospital: 'During my stay in the hospital I treated many people who had been beaten and shot by the Boers. Some of them were just shepherds and cattle herders, but they were accused of being SWAPO terrorists'.[40]

A Namibian nurse, Rauna Nambinga, gave detailed evidence to the *International Commission of Inquiry into the Crimes of the Racist and Apartheid Regime in Southern Africa* of the severe torture she had endured at the hands of the South African security police and army during two separate periods of detention. She had been detained for allegedly assisting SWAPO guerillas.[41]

The circumstances under which civilian medical personnel are obliged to work would seem to have contributed to the steadily deteriorating health conditions among the black population of Namibia.

Guns Pointed at Labour

Namibian workers have been faced with an ever-narrowing choice as the whole of Namibian society has become militarised under South African occupation. Traditionally, the majority of black workers have been forced to seek employment as migrant labourers in the white-owned industries, mines and farms, at starvation wages. The threat of conscription, the increased presence of armed police at workers' compounds, and the destruction of the economy in the north of the territory, where the majority of the migrant workers come from, have imposed an insoluble dilemma on those trying to make a living. If they remain in the 'white' industrial centres, they may find employment, but are exposed to frequent police raids on their places of residence, and arrest if they are found to be there 'illegally'. By returning to the north, they face almost certain destitution and the constant threat of South African army harassment.

Until 1977, a system of 'influx control' was in effect in Namibia under South African pass laws which made it illegal for a black person to remain in an urban area for longer than 72 hours without a permit. Africans had to carry passes and produce these on demand. A number of these 'pass laws' were abolished in October 1977, but many restrictions remained. Africans may still not seek, accept or remain in employment without official permission.[42] Identity cards, effectively replacing the 'pass', were introduced in November 1979.[43]

Police raids on workers' compounds, ostensibly to root out 'illegal' residents, have become more frequent and involved increasing police violence as the militarisation process has advanced. They have become an integral part of South Africa's strategy to control political activities among the black population. The war in the north has resulted in a stream of refugees coming to the already over-crowded black towns near the 'white' urban centres, thus increasing the number of 'illegal' residents under constant threat of victimisation.

Unemployment has risen sharply. In August 1981, one economist estimated that there were about 75,000 unemployed in Namibia, and 40,000 underemployed; the unemployment rate was 18.1 per cent of the total labour force.[44] The Windhoek Labour Bureau had registered 1,133 people as unemployed in January 1981. This excluded those who had arrived as refugees from the war in the north.[45]

By remaining in a 'white' urban area, black workers face not only police harassment and unemployment, but possible conscription into the army. They are thus presented with the problem of whether to take these risks, or to return to the north where the chances of working have been further eroded by the war. They may in any case not have this 'choice', since they may face arrest during a police raid and be either deported to the north or conscripted.

The pressures generated by the war thus appear to have forced an increasing number of people into a permanent state of uncertainty. While many of those in the north may flee south to escape from the violence perpetrated by the security forces, once arrived, they may be forced to return north or face conscription. As a result of these pressures, many have seen no alternative but to go into exile.

Conscription

When compulsory military service was extended in January 1981 to include black Namibians between the ages of 16 and 25, men from the Kaokoland, Ovambo, Kavango and Caprivi 'population groups' were exempted from the first call-up. The official reason for this was that the numbers called up would otherwise exceed demand. Therefore these 'population groups' were instead requested to volunteer for service in the tribal battalions already in existence in their respective areas.[46]

There was considerable confusion whether exemption applied only to those resident in the northern region, or to all members of these 'population groups' including those resident in the 'white' urban centres. As a result, large numbers of contract workers were reported to have left the workers' hostel in Katutura outside Windhoek to return to their homes in the north, for fear of being conscripted. Many were believed to have crossed the Namibian border into Angola or Botswana.[47] An army statement subsequently confirmed that the call-up was 'selective', and that the Ovambo, Kavango, Kaoko and Caprivi sections of the population would 'not be subject to this selective call-up'.[48]

At the end of the first year of conscription for all races, however, an army statement appeared to reverse this policy; while people of these groups resident in their 'homelands' would still not be liable to call-up, 'those Ovambo-speaking and Kavango-speaking citizens resident in urban areas are subject to call-up'.[49] In December 1981, the officer commanding the SWA Territory Force (SWATF) warned that those evading national service would be prosecuted under the Defence Act.[50]

Raids on Workers' Compounds

Namibian workers have a long history of resistance against the apartheid system imposed by South Africa, and of active support for SWAPO. In 1971/72, migrant workers from Ovambo initiated a general strike which ended only when South African troops, specially flown to Namibia, engaged in mass arrests and wholesale repression, imposing martial law on the entire Ovambo region. For the South African authorities, workers' militancy and support for SWAPO continues to pose a constant threat, which has increasingly been countered by police and military actions against workers in the black townships.

In June 1979, for instance, 1,500 workers were arrested during a day-long raid on Katutura. While the police claimed that this was a routine 'clean-up' and had no political implications, several Katutura residents were apparently told by security force members that they were looking for SWAPO members. Newspapers commented that 'many, if not most workers at the Ovambo hostel, which was the first to be raided, support SWAPO'.[51]

In August 1980, a special permanent police force consisting of 50 Ovambo

Special Constables under the command of six white South African Police officers, was introduced at the Katutura workers' hostel. Their presence has been a constant source of friction and has provoked numerous clashes. Katutura residents have complained that

'Rifles are pointed daily at residents. Is the place a hostel or a military camp. . ? We who live in the compound are all workers, yet our place has become a prison'.[52]

Two workers were shot dead within one week in 1980 by Special Constables for failing to produce their identity documents.[53]

In a letter to the *Windhoek Observer,* one of the residents at the Katutura single quarters complained about police brutality during two raids on the black town, describing them as 'barbaric'. The second raid, in February 1981, was carried out at the 'mixed single quarters', an area of Katutura where workers from different regions reside, officially without their families. (Generally, each 'ethnic group' of workers is forced to live in a separate area of the township, but there are some 'mixed' quarters). Many of the workers had their families with them despite official prohibition. The writer described how he witnessed police officers punching a pregnant woman and butting an old man with a rifle.[54]

A serious incident at the workers' hostel in Orwetoni, the black township near Otjiwarongo, in August 1981, was dismissed by the authorities as ethnic 'faction fighting'. A chain of violent incidents was set in motion by the fatal stabbing of a Damara-speaking woman in the township; apparently one in a series of attacks on women. A number of reprisal attacks on the houses of Ovambo-speaking residents occurred, in the belief that the woman's killer was an Ovambo.

Tension in the township had run high, but appeared to have quietened down when a group of Damara-speaking security forces arrived at the Ovambo workers' compound. The inmates were told to assemble on a soccer field while their dormitories were searched, apparently for weapons. Without warning, 'a total of about 50 teargas bombs were hurled into the crowd of Ovambo-speaking labourers', according to one press report. Wearing gas masks, the security forces (not clearly identified as soldiers or police) set upon the defenceless workers, beating them indiscriminately. A large number were reported to have been taken to hospital. The newspaper report pointed out that none of the workers had acted aggressively when ordered to evacuate their compound, that the teargas attack was unprovoked, and that the batonwielding police had the cover of machine guns.[55]

Special Constables were involved in an armed attack on the Ovambo compound in Katutura in May 1982, which resulted in one dead and a large number of wounded. According to one press report, a group of Special Constables, most in civilian clothes, 'went on the rampage', indiscriminately attacking people with knives and sticks. Three residents told reporters that the Special Constables 'beat, arrest and kill our people without having to pay for it. Compound residents are taken away without being heard of again'. The attack was apparently sparked off during a card game involving some off-duty Special Constables and hostel residents. When one of the Constables lost all his money, a fight erupted, and other Special Constables, some in uniform and armed, began to attack people indiscriminately. The day after the incident, reporters witnessed a worker being assaulted by a Special Constable as he returned from work. Throughout the attack on the compound, white officials, including the compound manager, apparently witnessed the behaviour of the Special Constables without taking any action. One of the workers who was attacked later told reporters: 'This is a big matter. I think it was planned'.[56]

Thousands of workers were turned out of their beds at 5 a.m. by armed police during a raid on the Katutura Ovambo compound in June 1982, ostensibly to identify illegal residents. Each worker had to produce his identity card and meal ticket before being cleared and two police vans were loaded with workers who had been arrested. Throughout the operation, police were stationed in groups around the compound wall.[57]

In July 1982, the Windhoek City Council announced its decision to take over two hostel complexes in Katutura and offer them to the SWA Territory Force. This would result in over 7000 workers being made homeless, and a further tightening of control over Katutura residents.[58]

V A WAR OF TERROR

The presence of approximately 100,000 South African-controlled troops in a country with a population of one and a quarter million belies South Africa's description of the war as a conflict of low intensity. In reality, the entire black population of Namibia has become engulfed by an increasingly brutal military operation. It appears certain that, short of a settlement acceptable to it, South Africa's strategy is to continue the forcible occupation of Namibia by military means, against the will of the overwhelming majority of Namibians. Two major components of this strategy are the fight against PLAN, the armed wing of SWAPO, and the repression of the Namibian population through systematic campaigns of terror.

The counterproductive effect of these measures has been clearly demonstrated by responses from the Namibian people themselves, whose rejection of South Africa's presence in their country has been noted by many observers. In February 1982, for example, a delegation from the South African Council of Churches visiting Namibia found a virtually unanimous view expressed by black Namibians they spoke to that 'the large majority of the people support SWAPO'. This support was growing every day with the continued presence of the South African security forces, seen as an occupying army and much resented by the local black populace. According to the delegation's report, the black view was summed up by one Namibian who said: 'The South Africans are the terrorists, they terrorise our people'.[1]

Violence against the civilian population takes many forms. In addition to the systematic use of arbitrary detention, torture, stop-and-search campaigns and destruction of crops and property by the occupying troops and local collaborators, there has also been an increasing number of atrocities committed by individual soldiers or police against civilians. In a number of instances these have involved the massacre of whole families or villages through random shooting, without provocation.

Systematic Terror

An increasing number of reports in the press and by foreign visitors have, in recent years, broken the wall of silence which surrounded the activities of the South African occupying army in Namibia. The reports point to a drastic escalation in the use of violence against civilians. In the words of one prominent American church leader visiting Namibia in 1979

> 'The evidence of South African army brutality among all segments of the population is so overwhelming, pervasive and capable of documentation that it makes a mockery of the South African government's claim to be "responding to the request of the Ovambo people for protection"'.

The visitor stressed that the primary source of the escalation of terror was without any doubt the South African army.

> 'It is the South African army, together with units of the Home Guard which detain and beat the students, hospital personnel and pastors, applying electric shock torture to those accused of aiding SWAPO. It is these who are responsible for harassing, intimidating, blackmailing and bribing the population. In the first instance it is they who deserve the name "terrorists"'.

The report gave as examples the cases of a teacher at Oshigambo bearing deep scars from a beating by 15 South African soldiers on the school grounds, of an emaciated doctor at the Engale Lutheran hospital being subjected to electric shock and 'drowning' with sand, of the wife of Bishop Kleopas Dumeni being forced, while under arrest, to dig out a latrine by South African soldiers and coerced to use it while being insulted by them.[2]

Countless incidents of this nature occur every day in the north of the country, and reports giving examples usually point out that these are merely the tip of the iceberg. One foreign visitor commented that during his short stay in northern Namibia in 1981, 'person after person told me of family members arrested, missing, or killed by the white South African army or security police'.[3]

A reporter from the *Windhoek Observer,* describing events in a small area of Ovambo during one week in November 1981, gave a picture of constant fear and terror inflicted on the local population. People were reluctant to talk to any stranger, but recurring stories of incidents during that week included the plundering of twelve shops and the torture of a number of people with electric shock by South African soldiers, a settlement razed to the ground, fences smashed and cars taken by soldiers.

In one reported incident armed men arrived at a cafe in a small settlement and opened fire on two teenagers. A man was taken to a nearby quarry and beaten by the soldiers, who demanded information about the youths. In another incident, military vehicles arrived during mass at a local church, and armed constables carried out searches on members of the congregation, ostensibly to find a man accused of having given a lift to a stranger. Two men and two women were severely beaten. One woman told the reporter of being approached by armed white men demanding to know about 'young men' who had allegedly slept at her shop some time earlier. When she denied any knowledge of this, she was blindfolded, subjected to electric shock torture and repeatedly raped.

In each case, the journalist gave the names of the victims and other details of the incidents. He concluded that 'these are just some of the incidents. It is well nigh impossible for a single reporter to cover the true extent of the atrocities'.[4]

The findings of the reporter were borne out by similar accounts by the leader of the Namibian Christian Democratic Party, Hans Röhr. Speaking in November 1981 in the National Assembly debate on the Bill on Combatting

Terrorism *(see Chapter II)* he warned that the security forces misused their powers in the name of 'combatting terrorism'. He cited the case of a schoolteacher in Ovambo who had been reported to the security police by a local resident as having received guerilla training. Röhr said that 'the teacher was arrested, put on trial, ill-treated for three days and then released. Nobody tried to determine the truth. In fact, he had never left the country, and had regularly been seen in his area'.

Röhr described a number of other arbitrary actions by the security forces in Ovambo, and cited similar incidents in the Kavango region. In one incident, soldiers accusing residents at a settlement of having supplied food to guerillas proceeded to assault the women. Two women were arrested, and only returned weeks later. Both said they had been assaulted and one had a broken arm. Röhr stressed that the incidents he had described were only a few examples.[5]

In early 1982, Röhr and a party of French, South African and Namibian journalists again visted the north to investigate continuing reports of atrocities committed by the security forces. The reporters were told a number of incidents of arbitrary shootings, detention and torture. A 70-year old man was shot dead by members of the SADF for no apparent reason, while resting under a tree. Another man was killed by the SADF while he was taking milk to his children—again no reason could be found. In another case, a man was arrested ostensibly on suspicion of being an MPLA spy, taken for interrogation at an army base and severely beaten. He met other detainees, one of whom said he had been put in a 30 cm high cage. When released, the detainee was told not to mention his experiences to anyone.[6]

It is evident from these and other reports that such behaviour on the part of the security forces is widespread, systematic and deliberate. For the local population, it implies that no-one is safe, anyone can be picked up at random and find himself or herself completely at the mercy of the security forces.

Massacres

In addition to accounts of the harassment, detention and torture of individuals, there have been reports of systematic attacks on whole communities. In one incident in early 1981, the army was reported to have attacked a small settlement in the Oonghoodi area in Ovambo, killing eleven civilians. The soldiers claimed they were looking for SWAPO guerillas. A survivor gave evidence that in fact seven men, two women and two children killed in the attack had been eating a meal, and there were no guerillas present.[7]

Eight people were killed and 12 badly wounded when, in March 1981, an 18 year old black soldier indiscriminately opened fire with a machine gun on people in the small village of Omashaka in Ovambo. According to an eyewitness, the people had been sitting outside their hut when there were sudden bursts of fire.[8]

A mass grave was reported by SWAPO to have been discovered in an area near Okatope, 25 miles from the Angolan border. According to sources inside Namibia, truckloads of people and corpses were taken to the place which had been cordoned off by South African troops.[9]

In January 1982, South African soldiers were reported to have opened fire on a crowd of people celebrating a wedding in a village in the north. 15 people were killed and 37 seriously wounded, according to SWAPO.[10]

Evidence of a massacre of eight people in a small village near Oshikuku in the north came to light in August 1982. The incident, which had occurred in March 1982, was the subject of an inquest in July, which ruled that the killings had been committed by 'terrorists', meaning SWAPO guerillas. Eyewitness accounts published in a Namibian newspaper claimed that the massacre had been carried out by armed soldiers of the SADF, who had lined the villagers up against a wall and summarily shot them. One of the survivors insisted that he had recognised one of the soldiers as a notorious Koevoet commander.[11]

On The Rampage

A number of particularly vicious killings involving members of the security forces have come to light in recent years, demonstrating the dehumanising effect of the army on individuals. Such cases show the contempt in which the occupying forces hold the lives of Namibians. Sentencing has often been light and 'mitigating circumstances', such as the military's task to kill, have been cited in court.

The following are examples of a large number of reported cases — it would seem likely that many other cases never reach the courts because of relatives' fears of reprisals.

In one case reported in early 1981, a member of the Police Special Task Force, Nagel, shot dead a black man because he called Nagel a boer.[12] The assailant was acquitted of murder and sentenced to six years imprisonment, three of which were suspended, for culpable homicide. In mitigation the judge said that it was Nagel's training which made him react with 'lethal efficiency'. Giving evidence for the defence, a psychologist declared Nagel to be normal but said 'it would be unlikely that members of the Task Force would be "good boys". The qualities of a good soldier meant that such a boy would have to have psychopathic and sociopathic tendencies'.[13]

In another case, three security guards of the State Electricity Corporation assaulted a black man, Moses Namiseb, whom they had encountered by chance as they were driving around the power station in Windhoek. Namiseb suffered heavy blows with a rifle and other attacks. He was found unconscious and died the next day. The autopsy report showed that he had 11 head injuries and 14 body injuries. The three accused reportedly showed amusement in court when evidence was given that the victim was found covered in blood and without his trousers on. One was sentenced to R400 or four months imprisonment, the other two to R600 or six months imprisonment.[14]

A 22-year old serviceman was sentenced to 10½ years imprisonment in January 1982 for raping a pregnant woman, using an army and a police vehicle without permission, housebreaking, theft and arson, all committed in July 1981. The accused told the court that he had committed the crimes out of boredom.[15]

A similar reason was given by an Ovambo Home Guard who machine-gunned eight men and women at a small village in Ovambo in March 1981. Two witnesses said the accused, Phillipus Augustus, had fired at people without any apparent reason. When asked why he had shot the people, Augustus replied that he was 'fed up'.[16]

A particularly gruesome case was brought before the Windhoek Supreme Court in early 1982, involving two South African soldiers aged 22 and 19. They were part of a group of soldiers who, in April 1981, cordoned off a settlement of workers, raided a house and demanded sexual intercourse from the women present. When the women refused they searched the premises and assaulted one man, Claudino Justino, whom they forced to take them to a 'SWAPO hide-out'. On the way they encountered two other men, whom they arrested for allegedly breaking the night curfew. The two South African soldiers then inflicted brutal torture on their two captives, pushing burning cigarettes in their nostrils and kicking them on the ground. One of the soldiers, Diedericks, continuously assaulted his victim to the extent that the other soldier intervened. Justino, who had stayed nearby, described in court how he could hear the terrified screams of the two captives. The soldiers concealed one of the dead victims in a drainage pipe and covered the other, who could still be heard breathing, with grass.[17] The men received sentences of 20 and 16 years imprisonment.

Rape

Namibian women are particularly vulnerable to police and army brutalities, facing the additional trauma of being raped. Numerous such incidents have been reported; in most cases the soldiers receive a very light sentence or a fine.

In one case reported in 1980, a 26-year old South African soldier, Johannes Pretorius, raped an 80-year old woman, Sabina Kasiku, at a wedding party in Kavango. Ms. Kasiku subsequently spent two weeks in hospital because of profuse bleeding. Evidence was presented that Pretorius had attempted to rape a younger woman first. Nevertheless, Pretorius' plea of innocence on the grounds that Kasiku had consented was accepted in court. He told a court reporter after the trial that he had lied to escape 'the shadow of the gallows'.[18]

An 18 year old South African soldier was given a suspended sentence for raping a black woman and attempting to rape another in February 1980. He only changed his plea to guilty after several women had given evidence.[19] A pregnant woman was reported to have died after being raped by five South African soldiers during an attack on civilians in September 1981.[20]

Faced with lenient attitudes towards such crimes, many women are reluctant to seek redress in court. A letter to the *Windhoek Observer* pointed out that

> 'South African Defence Force members in the north believe that they are free to do anything with an Ovambo-speaking person. Many women have been raped, and ... people killed like flies without compensation to their families. If the convicted cannot be punished according to the law, why bring them before the court?'[21]

Disappearances

An increasingly common occurrence, especially in the north of Namibia, has been the mysterious disappearance of people, either after having been detained, or simply in the course of their daily lives. There are no accurate statistics for the number of people who have disappeared, since families frequently do not report to the police if one of their relatives is missing, for fear of being themselves harrassed by the security forces. However, reports of such disappearances have from time to time been published. In 1980, a United Nations Working Group on Enforced and Involuntary Disappearances began to conduct inquiries into such cases all over the world.

There are also an unknown number of PLAN combatants held by the SADF, some captured during armed clashes, others during South African incursions into Angola. South Africa has released virtually no details about these captives, and refuses to accord them prisoner of war status under the Geneva Conventions. A few captured guerillas have been presented to the press in recent years, and occasional remarks by SADF officers indicate that these prisoners are used to obtain information on the strategy and tactics of PLAN. It is highly likely that they are subjected to physical and psychological pressures for this purpose. For instance, in July 1981, the head of the SWATF explained that in the past, the SADF had 'made use of' PLAN combatants. He refused to say how.[22]

Virtually nothing is known about the fate of injured PLAN combatants taken prisoner by the SADF. The International Red Cross has been denied access, and has expressed concern about the lack of information. A representative of the Windhoek Office of the Red Cross, expressing his concern about this in August 1981, said he was not even informed if there were any wounded PLAN prisoners held by the SADF. He stressed that

> 'it simply does not happen in any conflict or battle that you have a clash with 200 people and 45 are killed and no prisoners or wounded are taken'.[23]

SWAPO has periodically attempted to compile lists of people who had been described as 'missing' but had in fact been arrested. A SWAPO member responsible for compiling lists in northern Namibia reported one case in a letter in 1977. Soldiers had arrived at a local residence and taken the husband to a military camp. When the wife enquired after her husband, they responded with laughter, claiming that they had sent the man home. She was told by a black worker at the camp that he had seen the South African soldiers kill her husband the previous night and burn the body.[24]

The wives of three men who disappeared without trace in Ovambo in May 1979 brought an urgent application before the Windhoek Supreme Court in October, seeking the immediate release of their husbands from detention. The three men, Johannes Nakawa, Mathias Ashipembe and Mathias Nahanga were arrested on separate occasions; in each case the Defence Force authorities and police claimed that they had not detained the men and did not know of their whereabouts.[25] Nothing has been heard of the men since.

The disappearance and likely death under torture of another man, Johannes Kakuva, was the subject of a court case in 1981. A number of former political detainees filed affidavits with the Windhoek Supreme Court giving detailed evidence of torture and assault by the security police, and claiming that Kakuva, one of 25 people arrested in August 1980, died as a result. The security forces claimed that Kakuva, having agreed to act as a police informer, had absconded after having been taken to a prearranged spot to make contact with SWAPO guerillas. However, a fellow detainee claimed in his affidavit that he was present during Kakuva's torture by police, and witnessed his death.[26]

In 1982, SWAPO's London office gave the names of three other people reported missing: two teachers and a worker at the Lutheran Church press at Oniipa. All had been kept in detention. According to SWAPO, the regime claimed that the three men had escaped from prison, but no one knew their whereabouts.[27]

Military Inquiry

The numerous documented reports of army and police brutality have led to efforts by the SADF to improve its image. In March 1982, it announced the setting up of a military board of inquiry to investigate complaints.[28] The Head of the SADF in Namibia claimed that it was not army policy to condone such atrocities. 'The soldiers are here for the protection of the people', he said, 'not to act against them'. At the same time he claimed that reports of army brutalities were 'twisted propaganda' to whip up feelings. It was unthinkable that the disciplined South African soldiers would ill-treat the very people they were supposed to protect.[29]

The cosmetic nature of the inquiry quickly became clear from the composition of the Board, and from its failure to take effective action. The Board appeared to consist entirely of army personnel, headed by a Brigadier. During three months of investigations, it investigated 40 allegations of

Massacre at Oshikuku—March 1982

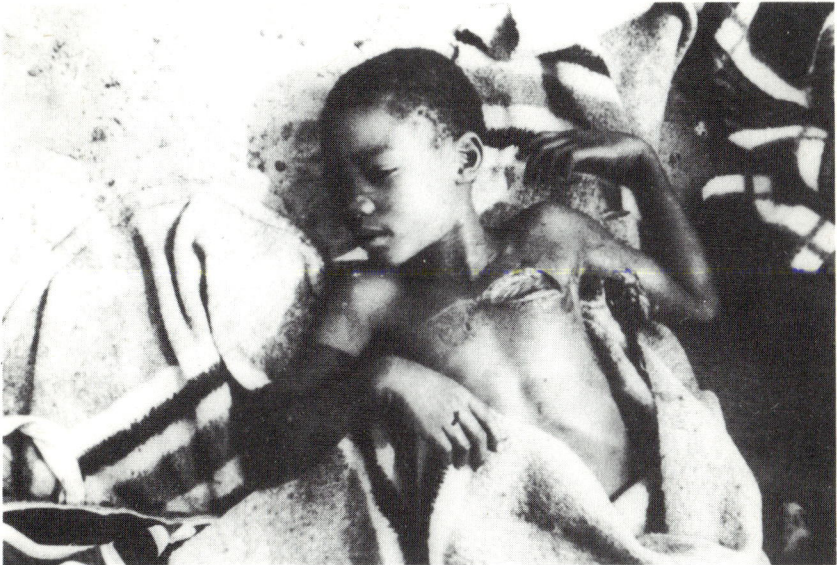

Eight people were killed, including children.

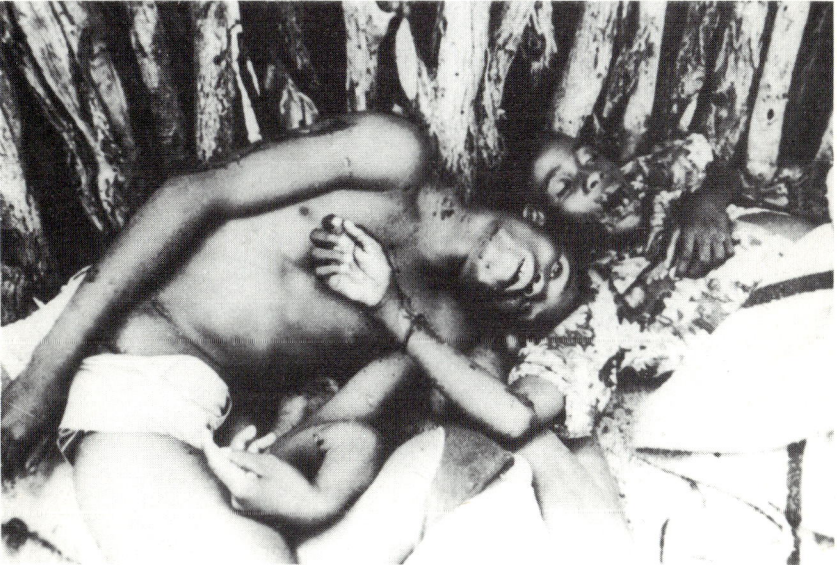

Villagers were lined up against the wall. . . .

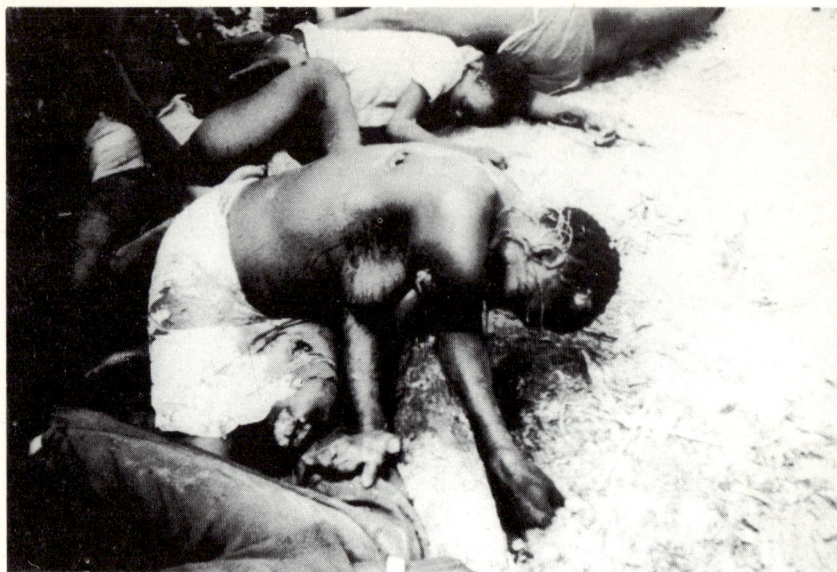

. . . .they were summarily shot.

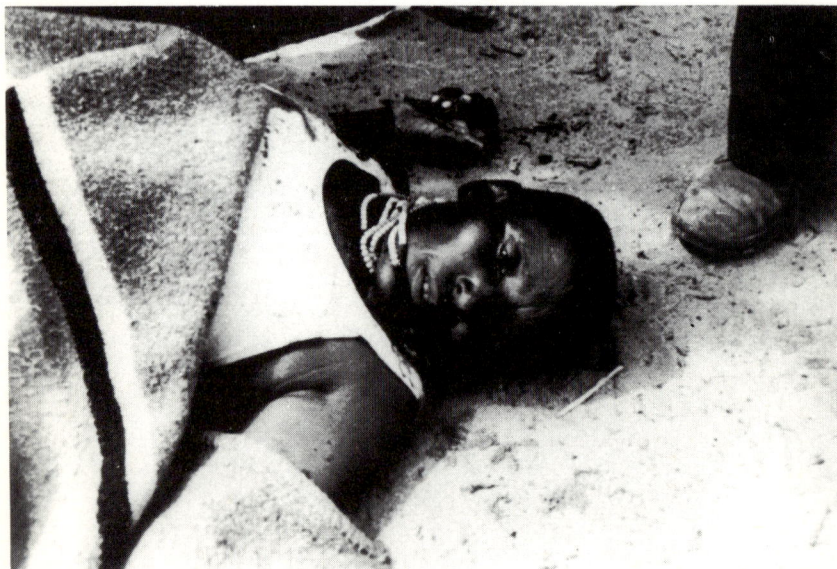

Villagers took photographs after the massacre.

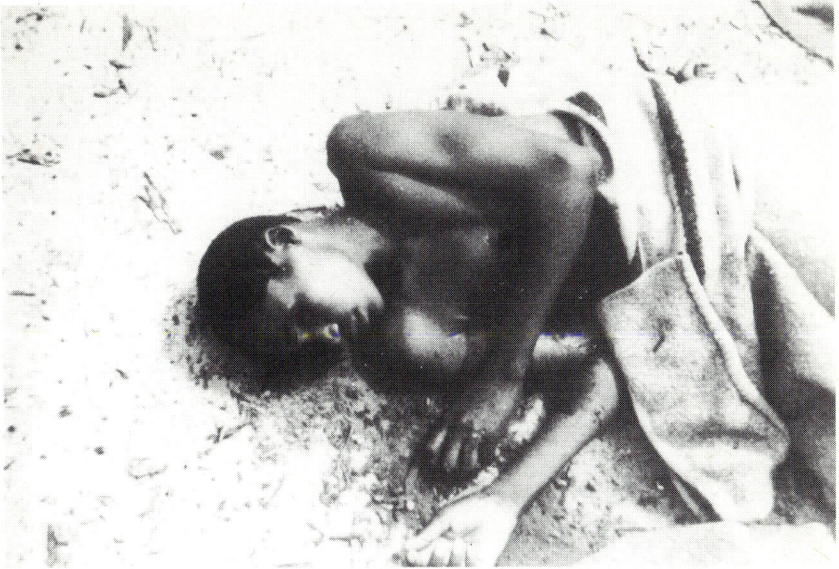

A survivor recognised the attackers as members of Koevoet.

There have been several reported massacres in Namibia.

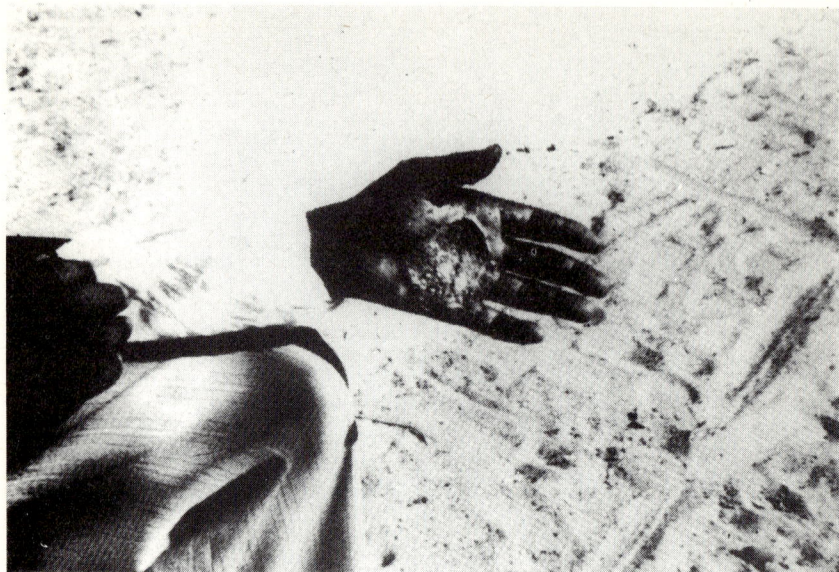

Brutality is widely used against civilians. A youth's hand, severely burnt, after being forcibly held against the exhaust of an army vehicle.

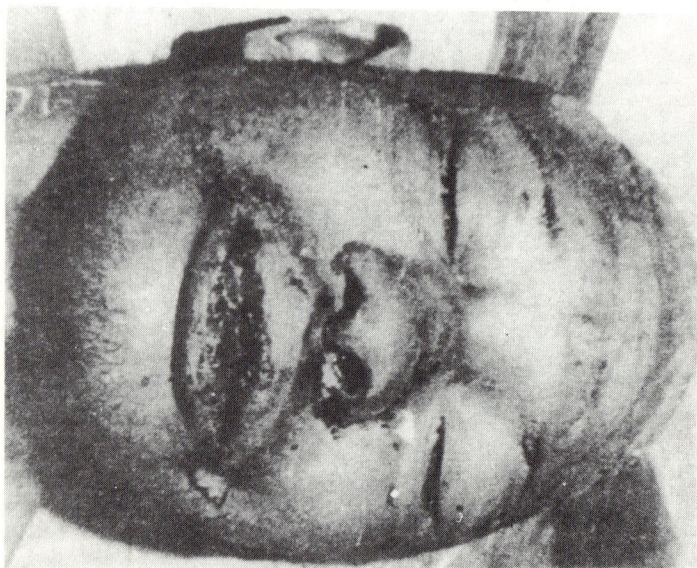

Moses Namiseb was beaten to death by three white security guards.

Three PLAN combatants on trial in the Windhoek Supreme Court.

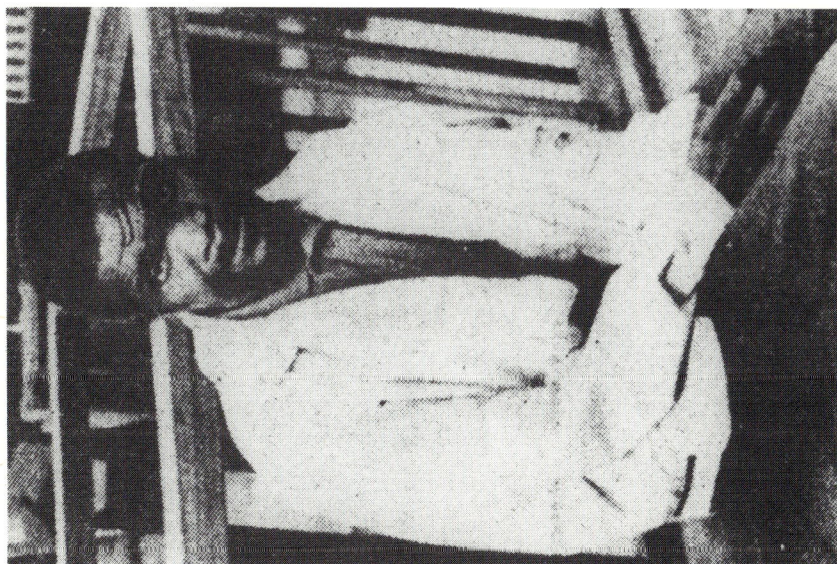

Markus Kateka, a farm worker, sentenced to death in 1980 for allegedly assisting SWAPO guerillas. His sentence was later commuted to 17 years imprisonment on appeal.

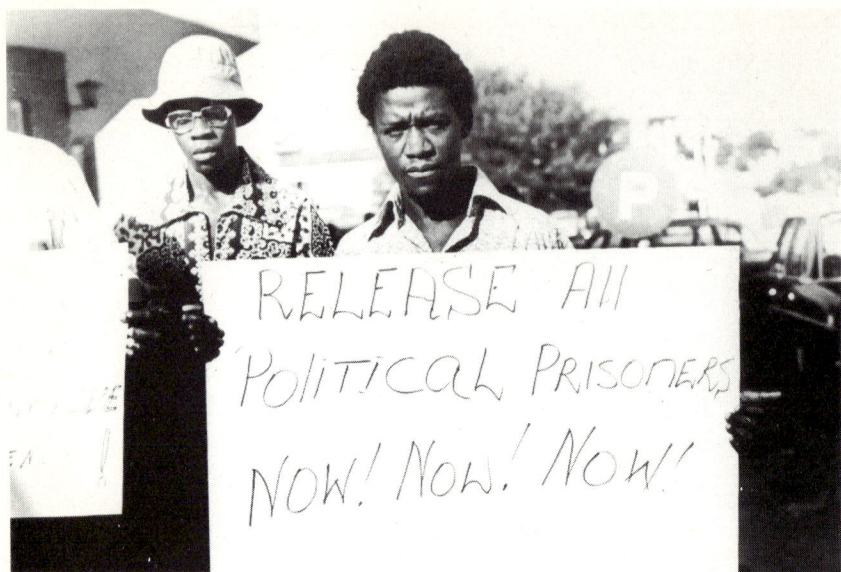

Depite repression, SWAPO in Namibia continues to protest against South Africa's occupation.

Herman Toivo ja Toivo, a founder member of SWAPO who is serving a 20 year prison sentence on Robben Island.

Immanuel Gottlieb Nathaniel Maxuilili Acting President of SWAPO inside Namibia, has been under banning orders in Walvis Bay since 1959.

Weighing children at SWAPO Health and Education Centre, Kwanza Sul, Angola.
Pic: Joost Guntenaar

SWAPO School at the Health and Education Centre, Kwanza Sul, Angola.
Pic: Joost Guntenaar

Sam Nujoma, President of SWAPO

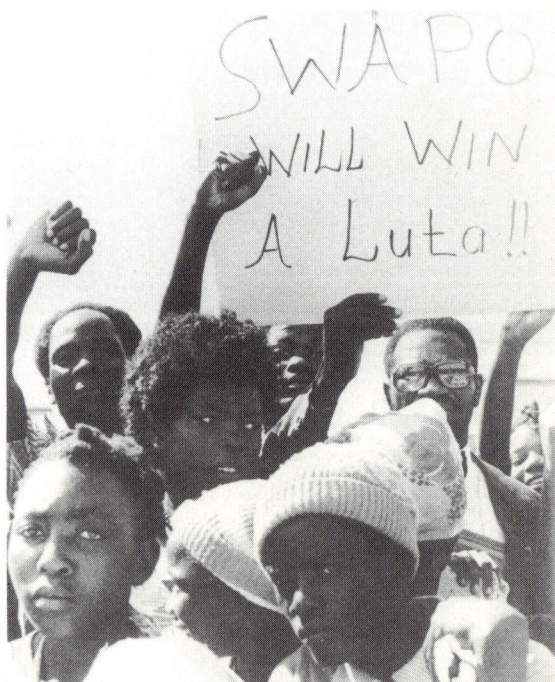

A SWAPO rally in Namibia.

security force atrocities. In most cases 'lesser transgressions were settled locally to the satisfaction of all concerned', the SADF claimed. 'It was not necessary to refer a single case to the Attorney General'. Some prosecutions would take place in some cases, and one man had already appeared in court, an SADF statement released in June 1982 said. No details of the incidents or the identities of the people involved were released.[30]

The officer commanding SWATF announced 'comprehensive measures' in June 1982 to combat incidents of alleged atrocities by members of the security forces. These included the setting up of communication links between the SWATF and the tribal 'governments', and the creation of a permanent military law office to investigate complaints.[31] A liaison committee had also been set up in the operational area by civilians and the SADF, according to a South African military official, involving Ovambo tribal officals, local businessmen, church members and Defence Force Commanders.[32] Comments by these military officials on announcing such measures made it clear, however, that they were mainly a public relations exercise, while the true extent of army brutality was being denied. One official claimed that 'considering the conditions and the number of troops, the rate of atrocities is very, very low', and that some allegations were 'typical, well-planned propaganda'. Soldiers now had to sign a special card stating that they respected the local population and would never resort to using physical violence against local inhabitants.[33]

These measures would seem to fall far short of creating a feeling of security among the local inhabitants. As the head of the Southern African Catholic Bishops' Conference, Archbishop Hurley, pointed out in an interview, people were unwilling to expose themselves by coming forward with complaints. During his visit to Namibia, he found people were only prepared to speak on the understanding that their names would not be revealed, fearing reprisals. He denied that ELOC had agreed to be represented on the army's investigation committee, on the grounds that the church was unwilling to give credibility to a body where the army was both accused and judge.[34]

VI THE PROPAGANDA WEAPON

The South African government has always justified its military occupation of Namibia by claiming that the SADF is in the territory at the request of the Namibian people, and that its role is the protection of the local population.[1] In an effort to promote this image internationally and locally, it has engaged in extensive propaganda activities. These are aimed at presenting the South African troops in Namibia as 'friends of the people' who help to maintain and improve the social welfare of the population, and at discrediting SWAPO by attributing all kinds of atrocities to the liberation movement. There is abundant evidence, however, that both planks in this policy have failed, and that the great majority of black Namibians resent army interference in their social structures, while identifying with SWAPO guerillas as friends, relatives and the liberators of Namibia.

The 'Hearts and Minds' Campaign

From the mid-1970s, South Africa stepped up its 'civic action' programme in Namibia, placing an increasing number of South African white national servicemen in schools, hospitals, agricultural units and other services, particularly in the north of the country. In May 1975, a South African official stated that more than 100 soldiers were already engaged in teaching, providing technical and agricultural advice, working as surgeons and vets in the Ovambo and Kavango regions, and that increased assistance from the SADF would probably swell that number to several hundred in the next few years.[2]

By 1977, the programme was well underway. Articles appeared in the South African press, particularly in *Paratus,* the journal of the SADF, on the success of the 'civic action' programme. One article described the vital role of soldiers in education, another stressed the army's assistance to people in the Caprivi, providing transport, food and medical services.[3] Another newspaper wrote of soldiers training black farmers, teaching blind children and operating government computers. In Ovambo, the soldiers filled key positions and ran essential services. At the hospital in Ondangwa, soldiers filled 12 of the 22 medical posts.[4]

The South African Administrator General explained the motives for this activity at a press conference in May 1979. Counter-insurgency consisted to 80% of winning support from the people and 20% of winning the war against SWAPO, he said. In keeping with this philosophy, South African teachers, doctors, farmers and tradesmen were assisting the SADF. From Katima Mulilo in the east to Ruacana in the west there were teams of national servicemen at work. At one school in Kavango, all the teachers with the exception of the headmaster were South African soldiers. Soldiers were running forestry projects in the Caprivi, agricultural settlements in Kavango, schools in Ovamboland and clinics in the Kaokoveld.[5]

Contrary to South Africa's claims, the programme is reported to have created great resentment among Namibian civilians. Denied the opportunity to train in professional jobs, they find instead armed soldiers taking over their social institutions. At one school, 700 students went on strike to protest against the recruitment of soldiers as teachers. Their parents formed the Black Parents Society to oppose the use of army personnel in Namibian schools.[6] A white nursing administrator, speaking about the deprivation of Namibia's already inadequate health services for black people, stressed that people in the north were forced to rely on army doctors provided by the SADF because they could not move about freely. While they had no choice, they did not welcome army doctors, she said.[7]

There was a strong view among visitors to the region in 1981 that the civic action programme had been an almost total failure in Ovamboland, and had not fared much better in the rest of the north.[8] The churches, in particular, were rejecting assistance from the SADF, not wanting to be identified in the eyes of Namibians with the occupying force. Similarly, school inspectors would not travel by official transport nor accept army escort. The image of anything official or connected with the army was considered either too hateful or too dangerous.[9] One SADF officer admitted that in Ovamboland 'I'm not sure it (the civic action programme) does much good because of the large number of SWAPO infiltrators'.[10]

Anti-SWAPO Campaign

The second strand of South Africa's propaganda war has been to conduct smear campaigns against the liberation movement, SWAPO. The national and international press rely almost entirely on South African information when reporting events in Namibia. Reports in the South African and Namibian press are subject to censorship, and travel in the north of the territory is only possible with permission from the military authorities. These restrictions give the SADF the opportunity to feed reports to the press, which present SWAPO as the aggressor, engaged in atrocities and with very little support among the local population. For example, an article in a pro-South African government newspaper reported in June 1980 that 'the military authorities in the Kavango and Caprivi believe the local population almost totally reject SWAPO'.[11] Another newspaper reported in September 1979 that 'a band of terrorists' had set fire to a kraal in Ovamboland and thrown a 13 year old boy into the flames.[12]

Following the disclosure of South African propaganda activities by the South African Department of Information in 1978, evidence was published of 'Operation Cherry', a clandestine radio campaign designed to discredit SWAPO by broadcasting faked SWAPO messages from a ship operating off the Namibian coast. £600,000 had been allocated for anti-SWAPO propaganda operations in Namibia.[13]

In November 1979, the South African government published one-page advertisements in major Western newspapers depicting SWAPO as 'terrorists' and accusing the movement of committing atrocities and indiscriminate killings in Namibia.[14]

South Africa's propaganda tactics in Namibia appear to have had little effect on the attitude of the majority of the black population, though the regime's international campaigns, through propaganda agencies placed in Western capitals and misinformation fed to the press, have frequently resulted in a distorted picture being presented to the Western public. Statements from Namibians themselves, and reports by visitors, indicate that the Namibian people are very clear about who commits atrocities, and about whom they support. A chief in Kavango, speaking to a group of journalists in February 1981 of the death of his two children when a landmine exploded near his farm, said 'SWAPO would never have done this'.[15]

A delegation from the British Council of Churches were told by local people that SWAPO guerillas operated in the areas where they were known, they explained their actions to the local people, and thus what they did was predictable and understood. It was true that they placed mines, the delegation was told. It was true that they killed people, but these were normally informers. According to local residents, when SWAPO guerillas approached a farmstead for food, if they were not known and were refused, they left peacably. It was those who pretended to be SWAPO who used violence in order to demand food.[16]

A Namibian woman, Ida Jimmy, was gaoled for seven years in October 1980 for expressing publicly what most Namibians appear to believe:

> '. . . we are always told not to accept the freedom fighters. As the boers say, "terrorists" . . . so called terrorists must not be given food. Or if you give a terrorist a sleeping place then you must suffer for that action.
>
> 'There is no terrorist. . . These are our sons that leave the country. . . so fellow comrades give the freedom fighters food. Give them sleeping places so that they can go forward and carry out their tasks. They are not terrorists, they are your children. They do not come to murder you, but to save you from the oppression of the South African boer regime'.

She attacked South African propaganda which concealed the losses it suffered in armed encounters with SWAPO or presented the corpses of black members of the South African armed forces as those of SWAPO combatants. The SADF was not protecting people in northern Namibia. It did not care about sick patients, or old people. 'They intimidate those people and torture them until they are dead'.[17]

A practice which appears to be frequently used by the local recruits of the SADF is to disguise themselves as SWAPO guerillas while committing atrocities against civilians, and subsequently claim that these were committed by SWAPO. In one reported case, for instance, a shopkeeper in Rundu was repeatedly visited by a man in a uniform not usually worn by South African security forces, and armed with an AK47 rifle, the type attributed to SWAPO guerillas. The man kept asking questions about a Mr. Mbanzi, another local resident. The shopkeeper recognised the armed man as someone residing at the living quarters at the local secondary school and, on making inquiries, found a group of men there. Their leader admitted that they were members of the security forces whose task it was to make night visits to people who were enemies of the DTA. He reportedly also admitted that it was the group's work to terrorise people, masquerading as SWAPO guerillas, in an effort to frighten them and to make the allegations of SWAPO 'terrorism' more credible. He justified the group's action by saying they were 'only working for their bread' and that this was their only income.[18] Soldiers disguised as SWAPO guerillas were claimed by eyewitnesses to be responsible for a massacre near Oshikuku in northern Namibia *(see Chapter V)*.

VII INTO EXILE

As one option after another is being closed to Namibians of all ages under South Africa's military occupation, an increasing number have been forced into exile. They have fled from the constant surveillance of South African security forces, the experiences of repression, attacks on their property, and the ever present threat of torture and death. In their own country, they have been deprived of adequate education and health care, seeing these services break down completely in the north as a result of the war. They have been forced to go into exile to gain an opportunity of building the sort of community they wish to live in.

By September 1981, an estimated 73,000 Namibians, or nearly six per cent of the population, had fled into exile.[1] Many have left relatives and friends behind.

Between June 1974 and early 1975, over 6,000 people left Namibia. They fled from an intensified campaign of terror in the north, which included public floggings of SWAPO supporters who had boycotted the Ovambo tribal elections held in 1973.[2] Refugee settlements were set up in Zambia and, after Angolan independence, in Angola. In mid-1978, there were between 2,500 and 3,000 Namibian refugees at a settlement in Nyango in Zambia, adminstered by SWAPO. The settlement included a creche, clinic and schools as well as livestock and agricultural projects and training workshops for skills such as carpentry.[3]

Since 1975, increasing numbers of refugees have fled to Angola. In May 1978, a refugee settlement at Kassinga in southern Angola was bombed by the South African forces, and troops massacred over 600 refugees and wounded over 1,000. Between 200 and 300 Namibians were captured, and 118 of those were still being held in detention in Namibia in 1982. A new settlement was provided by the Angolan government in Kwanza Sul, where the majority of Nambian refugees have been accommodated.

A mass exodus began in late 1980, as a direct result of the introduction of compulsory military service in Namibia. By July 1981, an additional 20,000 Namibians were reported to have arrived in Angola.[4]

The arrival of such large numbers has stretched the resources of the refugee settlements almost beyond the limit. SWAPO officials administering the settlements were faced with shortages of all basic essentials, such as tents, blankets, water, etc. One SWAPO official described how busloads of children were arriving every day at the main refugee settlement in Angola, Kwanza Sul; on one occasion six busloads arrived in one day.[5]

Many of the refugees are in ill-health, and may be in a state of shock from experiences in Namibia. Having made the arduous and dangerous journey to Angola, they would then have spent several weeks at various SWAPO transit camps before arriving at Kwanza Sul.

Once in exile, a new life begins, which although full of hardship and material deprivation, nevertheless offers a freedom from oppression that has never before been experienced by the refugees, together with opportunities to create a new way of life in preparation for an independent Namibia. While some refugees join SWAPO's armed wing, PLAN, and others are sent abroad to other African countries or overseas, the majority remain in the refugee settlements. Here SWAPO has established a basic infrastructure which is aimed at providing the sort of care, education and political environment which will enable Namibians to rebuild their country when South Africa has been forced to withdraw.

Projects in health care, education, adult literacy, craft training, agriculture, etc., are being carried out with assistance from sections of the international community. In Kwanza Sul, members of the SWAPO Women's Council have developed a maternity and childcare centre, a kindergarten and a training programme for nurses and midwives in conjunction with the SWAPO health authorities. Education is regarded as an important priority and a complex of schools has been set up in the refugee settlements, with temporary schools in the transit camps. There is a strong emphasis on subjects of practical relevance — mathematics, chemistry, physics and natural sciences, hygiene, geography, history and politics. In Kwanza Sul, there were 10,000 schoolchildren in December 1981, with 53 teachers.

In addition, an adult literacy programme has been established, using those already literate to teach others. Other training includes courses in electrical engineering, carpentry, medicine, nutrition, childcare and other subjects.[6]

Under the difficult conditions of exile and material shortages, and with the assistance of their host governments in Angola and Zambia, the Namibian people in exile are preparing for their return to a free Namibia.

In the occupied territory itself, the black majority's desire for independence, peace and a society based on racial equality is being daily violated by South Africa's illegal occupation. From the evidence of suffering inflicted on the Namibian population, it is abundantly clear that the withdrawal of South Africa's troops and administration, and the holding of United Nations-supervised elections, are the only way to achieve the goal desired by most Namibians.

REFERENCES

The following abbreviations are used:

BBC British Broadcasting Corporation Monitoring Service

CT *Cape Times,* Cape Town

Cit *The Citizen,* Johannesburg

DD *Daily Despatch,* East London

DN *Daily News,* Durban

Focus *Focus* on Political Repression in Southern Africa, IDAF news bulletin

FT *Financial Times,* London

IHT *International Herald Tribune,* New York

LWI *Lutheran World Information,* Geneva

MS *Morning Star,* London

NYT *New York Times,* New York

RDM *Rand Daily Mail,* Johannesburg

SExp *Sunday Express,* Johannesburg

SExp(Lon) *Sunday Express,* London

ST *Sunday Times,* Johannesburg

ST(Lon) *Sunday Times,* London

Star *Star,* weekly airmail edition, Johannesburg

S. Tel *Sunday Telegraph,* London

Tel *Daily Telegraph,* London

T *The Times,* London

WA *Windhoek Advertiser,* Windhoek

WO *Windhoek Observer,* Windhoek

INTRODUCTION

1. *Apartheid's Army in Namibia – South Africa's illegal military occupation,* IDAF, January 1982; population figures are based on a census conducted by South Africa in May 1981. Independent sources give the Namibian population as higher. A study published by the United Nations Institute for Namibia in 1978 estimated the Namibian population at 1,250,000. *Towards Manpower Development for Namibia – Background Notes,* United Nations Institute for Namibia, 1978, P.1.
2. *WO* 21.3.81.
3. Paul A. Wee, General Secretary, Lutheran World Ministries, New York, *Notes on Namibia,* 14.8.79
4. Interview with Dr. Iyambo Indongo, SWAPO Secretary for Health and Social Affairs, at Kwanza Sul Settlement, *Focus Special Issue No. 2,* April 1981
5. *Report on Namibia,* the Southern African Catholic Bishops' Conference, May 1982, p.21.
6. *ibid.*
7. *Focus* No. 36, September/October 1981, p.4.
8. A representative from the American Friends' Services Committee, visiting Namibia in 1981, was told by a white official that 'at least 90 per cent of the population of Namibia are loyal to SWAPO'. *Southern Africa,* March/April 1981.
9. For information about South Africa's political strategy in Namibia, see *Namibia–the Facts,* IDAF, 1980.

CHAPTER I

1. *Report from the War Zone,* account by a member of the Toronto Committee for the Liberation of Southern Africa of a visit to Namibia in February 1981, in: TCLSAC Report, April 1981.

2. *Apartheid's Army in Namibia,* op. cit., p. 12.
3. *Focus* No. 37, November/December 1981, pp. 8-10.
4. *Apartheid's Army in Namibia,* op. cit., pp. 11-13.
5. *Military activities and arrangements by colonial powers in territories under their administration which might be impeding the implementation of the Declaration on the granting of independence to colonial countries and peoples: Namibia.* Working paper prepared by the UN Decolonisation Committee, A/AC. 109/660, 15.6.81, p.2.
6. *WA* 18.1.80, *WO* 15.12.79.
7. *Paratus,* May 1980.
8. *WO* 27.6.81
9. *ST* 17.8.80
10. *DD* 21.8.80
11. *ST* 17.8.80.
12. *T* 17.2.81.
13. Wee, *Notes on Namibia, op. cit.*
14. *Namibia, A Nation Wronged,* report of a visit to Namibia by a Delegation sent by the British Council of Churches at the Invitation of the Council of Churches in Namibia, Division of International Affairs, February 1981, p.13.
15. *RDM* 18.10.75.
16. *Focus* No. 2, January 1976, p.1.
17. *WA* 29.10.75.
18. *GN* 30.8.76; *ST* 4.9.76.
19. *GN* 1.9.76.
20. *WA* 8.7.76
21. *WO* 9.5.81
22. *The Combatant,* Vol. III, No. 10, April 1982.
23. *WO* 4.7.81.
24. *NYT* 15.1.81.
25. TSLSAC Report, *op. cit.*
26. *GN* 15.6.81.
27. *Southern African Information Programme* of the International University Exchange Fund, Bulletin, August 1978.
28. *NYT* 15.1.81.
29. *Tel* 30.7.81.
30. *WO* 5.12.81.
31. *WA* 22.1.82.
32. Wee, *op. cit.*
33. *WO* 9.2.80.
34. See Chapters IV and V for accounts of the activities of these units; for a detailed description of all the South African and Namibian security forces operating in Namibia, see Apartheid's Army in Namibia, *op. cit.*
35. *Star* 20.4.81.
36. *WO* 22.2.81
37. *Citizen* 2.2.81.
38. *ibid.*
39. *ibid.*
40. *Namibia Today,* Vol. 4, No. 5/6, 1980, p.24.
41. *WO* 29.11.80; *LWI* 22.1.81, 19.2.81.
42. *To the Point,* 5.12.80; see also Chapter IV.

CHAPTER II

1. A number of articles have been published in recent years supporting the view that SWAPO would win free elections in Namibia. In two consecutive articles in 1980, Dr. Gerhard Tötemeyer, a South African writer on Namibian affairs, expressed the view that SWAPO enjoyed majority support in the north of the country, and that this support also stretched deep into the south *(RDM 7.5.80).* A detailed study prepared by South African intelligence in April 1980 reportedly predicted that in a democratic election, SWAPO would probably win as much as 83 per cent of the votes. The reporter quoting this finding commented that this would not come as a surprise to outside observers *(New Statesman 22.8.80).*
2. *Focus* No. 16, May 1978, p.6.
3. *Focus* No. 20, January/February 1979, pp. 2-3.
4. *Focus* No. 22, May/June 1979, p.14.
5. *WO* 7.6.80.
6. *WA* 7.2.80.
7. Report by Lucia Hamutenya at a Conference in London, February 1980, organised by SATIS — South Africa, The Imprisoned Society.
8. *CT* 3.9.81; *WA* 3.9.81
9. *The Workers of Namibia,* IDAF, February 1979, Chapter VIII.
10. *Focus* No. 7, November 1976, p.14.
11. *The Combatant,* Vol. 2, No. 8, March 1981.
12. *Government Notice AG 8,* 6.2.80
13. *Star* 20.4.81.
14. *RDM* 14.5.79
15. *RDM* 7.11.79
16. *Star* 8.7.79.
17. *WO* 9.7.80.
18. *Citizen* 9.6.80.
19. *WA* 19.7.79.
20. *WA* 23.4.81.
21. *WO* 16.1.82.
22. *NYT* 15.1.81.
23. *Sowetan,* 24.2.82.
24. *WO* 4.4.81
25. *WO* 24.5.81.
26. *WO* 22.5.82; *WA* 17.5.82.
27. TCLSAC Report, *op. cit.*
28. *WO* 19.12.81.

CHAPTER III

1. *WO* 6.2.82.
2. *LWI* 4.3.82; *WA* 1.3.81.
3. *Namibia, A Nation Wronged,* BCC Report, *op. cit.*
4. *Report on Namibia,* published by the Southern African Catholic Bishops' Conference (SACBC), May 1982, *op. cit.*
5. *LWI* 4.3.82.
6. *Lutheran World Ministries Report* 19/20.11.80; *Focus* No. 33, March/April 1981, p.9; see also Chapters I and V on Koevoet.
7. *Focus* No. 6, September 1976 p.3.
8. *WO* 11.8.79.
9. *WO* 27.6.81.
10. *A Report about the visitation at Elombe parish,* 16.5.82, by Bishop Kleopas Dumeni.
11. *Star* 12.6.82.
12. *LWI* 17.6.82.
13. *T* 15.7.78.
14. *LWI* 10/80.
15. *WO* 29.8.81.
16. *WA.* 19.10.81.

CHAPTER IV

1. *Focus* No. 8, January 1977, p.14.
2. *Focus* No. 9, March 1977, p.16.
3. *DD* 9.12.76.
4. Interview with Filemon Itula, *Action on Namibia,* June 1982.
5. *WA* 17.5.82.
6. Interview with Naufiku Kaukungua, with a member of IDAF Research Department, 10.2.1980.
7. *WA* 15.3.76.
8. *GN* 1.9.76.
9. *Namibia Bulletin,* March 1980, p.8.
10. *WA* 6.10.80.
11. *RDM* 11.6.80.
12. *WA* 8.12.80.
13. *GN* 15.6.81.
14. *WO* 29.11.80.
15. *The Combatant,* February 1981, p.3.
16. *WA* 3.2.81.
17. *LWI* 3/81.
18. *WA* 18.5.82.
19. *WA* 15.12.80.
20. *S* 10.6.81.
21. *Report of the United Nations Council for Namibia,* Vol. I, 1974, p.8.
22. *Objective Justice,* United Nations Department of Public Information, Spring 1975.
23. *WO* 9.10.80.
24. *WA* 8.12.80.
25. *WA* 11.6.81.
26. *RDM* 11.6.80.
27. *Focus* No. 33, March/April 1981, p.9.
28. WA 15.4.82.
29. *WA* 9.6.82.
30. *NYT Magazine,* 1.8.82.
31. *WA* 11.6.81.
32. *WA* 15.4.82
33. *Paratus,* June 1978.
34. *WA 11.6.81.*
35. *WO* 4.10.80
36. *WO* 29.11.80; *Star* 27.12.80.
37. Statement by Bishop Kleopas Dumeni, 16.7.80.
38. *ibid.*
39. *The Combatant,* Vol II, No. 7, February 1981.
40. Testimony of a Kassinga survivor, in *Remember Kassinga and other papers on political prisoners and detainees in Namibia,* IDAF, July, 1981.
41. *ibid.*
42. *The Workers of Namibia, op. cit.*
43. *WO* 23.3.80.
44. *WA* 7.8.81.
45. *WO* 9.1.82.
46. *Focus* No. 33, March/April, 1981, p.6.
47. *WO* 13.12.80.
48. *ibid.*
49. *WO* 19.12.81.
50. *DN* 1.12.81.
51. *RDM* 2.7.79; *WO* 30.6.79; *FT* 27.6.79.
52. *WO* 23.8.80.
53. *WO* 23.3.80.
54. *WO* 28.3.81.
55. *WO* 15.8.81.
56. *WA* 10/11.5.82.
57. *WA* 24.6.82.
58. *WA* 27.8.82.

CHAPTER V

1. *Information,* Newsletter of the Council of Churches in Namibia, March 1982.
2. Wee, *Notes of Namibia, op. cit.*
3. *Terror in Namibia,* by J. Evenson, in *The Lutheran,* 18.2.81.
4. *WO* 19.12.81.
5. *WO* 28.11.81.
6. *WO* 27.2.82.
7. *ST(Lon)* 22.3.81.
8. *WO* 4.4.81.
9. *SWAPO Information and Comment,* Vol. 2, No. 5, August/September 1980.
10. *IHT* 26.2.82.
11. *WO* 28.8.82.
12. The term 'boer' refers to whites of Afrikaner descent. In this context, the term would be interpreted as an insult if used by a black person.

13. *WA* 27.2.81.
14. *WA* 19.5.81.
15. *WA* 13.1.82.
16. *WA* 25.11.81.
17. *WO* 3.4.82.
18. *Resister,* No. 11, December 1980, pp. 14-15.
19. *WO* 16.8.80.
20. *SWAPO Information and Comments,* Vol. 2, No. 9, December 1980.
21. *WO* 30.8.80
22. *DD* 17.7.81.
23. *Star* 18.8.81; see also *The Capture and Treatment by South African Forces of Combatants of the Peoples' Liberation Army of Namibia,* evidence submitted by the IDAF to the Ad Hoc Working Group of Experts of the United Nations Commission on Human Rights, London, 12.7.82.
24. *SWAPO Information and Comment,* Vol. 1, No. 3, September/October 1979.
25. *WA* 24/29.10.79; *WO* 27.10.79.
26. *WO* 9.1.82.
27. *SWAPO Information and Comment,* Vol. 4, No. 2, February/May 1982.
28. *WA* 15.3.82.
29. *WA* 2.3.82.
30. *CT* 5.6.82; *BBC* 7.6.82.
31. *WA* 9.6.82.
32. *ST* 30.5.82.
33. *ibid.*
34. *FM* 21.5.82.

CHAPTER VI

1. *WA* 2.3.82.
2. *BBC* 7.5.75.
3. *Paratus,* January 1977.

4. *WA* 3.10.77.
5. *RDM* 7.5.79.
6. *Sechaba,* June 1980.
7. *WA* 11.6.81.
8. *FT* 12.2.81; *T* 17.2.81.
9. *Report on Namibia,* by the Southern African Catholic Bishops' Conference, *op, cit.*
10. *FT* 12.2.81.
11. *Citizen* 9.6.80.
12. *RDM* 25.9.79.
13. *Obs* 25.3.79; *GN* 30.3.79.
14. *S Exp(Lon)* 11.11.79.
15. *WO* 27.2.82.
16. *Namibia, A Nation Wronged, op. cit.,* p. 13.
17. *Speech made by Ida Jimmy in Lüderitz on* 13.7.80, reproduced in *Focus* No. 34, May/June 1981, p.4.
18. *WO* 19.6.62.

CHAPTER VIII

1. *Focus* No. 36, September/October 1981, p.5.
2. *GN* 2.7.74.
3. *Report of a visit to the SWAPO Health and Education Centre, Nyango, Zambia,* 21.7.78, by D. de Beer.
4. *BBC* 13.7.81.
5. Report by Ellen Musialela, Secretary for Finance of SWAPO Women's Council, March 1982.
6. *Angola: Fighting Apartheid; Focus* Special Issue No. 2, April 1981; Information supplied by Libolius Haufiku, Head of Sports and Culture Department, Kwanza Sul, during a visit to London, 14.12.81.

INDEX